THE
LONDON
YEAR

THE

What to Do

LONDON

and When

YEAR

Yolanda Zappaterra & Sarah Guy

FRANCES
LINCOLN

Contents

Introduction

There's always something happening in London, but how often have you come across an event you'd love to attend, only to find it sold out months ago? Or missed Open House *yet again* because you didn't get your act together? Or realised too late that if you'd registered for an event just a month earlier you might have been able to go to it?

Because London is home to thousands of events, encompassing everything from stately ceremonial occasions to small, quirky happenings, and headline-grabbing tournaments to local knees-ups, it can be easy to miss out on things. But whether your interests lie in literature, music, gardening, sport, art, live performance, architecture, film, the natural world, food and drink, history, education or tradition, you'll find events of interest in these pages.

London offers grand spectacle, emotional moments and one-off occasions galore, but you have to book or apply for tickets for many of them – months in advance in the case of the Chelsea Flower Show or Wimbledon. *The London Year* is here to help you plan ahead so that you don't miss the boat.

The good news is that there's also plenty of room for spontaneity, with lots going on that requires little or no booking – just turn to a month in the book and take your pick from activities as varied as bluebell walks, the London to Brighton Veteran Car Run or the Greenwich+Docklands International Festival.

Smaller events like firework displays or cultural festivals are often free and easier to attend, but ticketed, meaning you need to know when the tickets are likely to be released or how to apply for them. Again, *The London Year* gives you the information you need to book. If you want to revel in the auditory feast that is the city's annual steelband competition, witness centuries-old ceremonies and recreations of medieval battles, know when to catch Richmond Park's rhododendrons in full bloom or the arrival of seasonal birds at the London Wetland Centre, *The London Year* is for you.

You don't need deep pockets to enjoy many of the occasions – watching hot air balloons float over London, admiring the Winter Lights displays or cheering on the rowers at the Great River Race are all tremendous fun for no cost. And there are little-known curiosities that are a joy to discover, such as the Blessing of the River Thames, or Cart Marking. Alongside eye-popping spectacles such as Trooping the Colour, there's peace and quiet to be had too – go snowdrop-spotting or retreat to the Ever After remembrance garden. The 200+ events, activities and attractions we've gathered together should offer something for readers of all ages, including many events and activities that even Londoners will be unfamiliar with or unaware of.

We hope *The London Year* shows you the range and depth of what the city has to offer, and inspires you to experience as many of the events as you can.

How the book works
Each entry that requires booking ahead or registration includes the organiser website at the top, and dates when tickets go on sale or registration opens at the bottom, signposting you to what you need to do. Entries are colour-coded to indicate the interest that they fulfil.

Sport

Culture/Lifestyle

Tradition/History

Natural World

Society

January

Make a hullabaloo in an orchard
Wassail Day

> wildlondon.org.uk

The ritual of wassailing has its roots in pagan Britain, when people would gather in orchards on Twelfth Night (5 or 6 January) to make lots of noise in the hope of scaring off bad spirits, thereby ensuring a good harvest for the year ahead. On **Wassail Day**, singing, dancing, chanting, lots of pot-banging and general merrymaking would ensue, and the noisy spirit banishers would be fuelled and rewarded with spiced cider, perry or ale, served from a communal wassail bowl provided by the orchard's grateful owner. While there aren't many orchards in London in which to experience this, the London Wildlife Trust's annual event at Dulwich's Village Orchard, usually in the third weekend of January, is a delightful affair, filled with live music, poetry, storytelling and more – including pinning toast to trees. Why? Well, go along and find out!

> *Tickets on sale in December*

Hit the new year running with a jog round Hyde Park
Serpentine New Year's Day 10k

> serpentine.org.uk

Zoom in on the short film scene
London Short Film Festival (LSFF)

> shortfilms.org.uk; straight8.net

London has hundreds of fundraising runs and park runs through the year, but the **Serpentine New Year's Day 10k** (there's also a 3k run for children and those nursing a hangover) in Hyde Park is a great way to kick off the new year, affording participants the smug feeling of having nailed their first 10k of it before lunchtime. Taking in Hyde Park and Kensington Gardens landmarks like Speakers' Corner, where Karl Marx and George Orwell once spoke, the rose garden and the Diana, Princess of Wales Memorial Fountain, it's a fun and inclusive event for all comers, though you'll need to sign up a month or so before the event to ensure a spot among the 650 runners. If you don't make it, the running and triathlon club Serpentine (which organises the event), has plenty of other options throughout the year, while Running Calendar UK is a great resource for runs of all distances and types, including many charity runs.

While the capital's glamour-filled, red-carpet film festival is the mammoth BFI London Film Festival held in October (see page 142), its smaller sibling, the **London Short Film Festival (LSFF)** still has the blessing of Britain's leading film organisations, BAFTA and BIFA, with films screened qualifying for entry in both their awards. A key date for emerging talent in the industry, the LSFF is held in the latter half of January, over ten days. Between 250 and 500 British and international films are screened in indie cinemas around the city, including the ICA, BFI, Garden Cinema and Curzon Soho in central London, the Genesis and Phoenix in the east and Brixton Community Cinema in the south. In addition, there are workshops, Q&As, panel discussions and more. The films, by creatives working in the visual arts, are as innovative as they are eclectic in their range of genres. For shorter films, the annual Straight8 competition, in which entrants must produce a one-cartridge, unedited Super8 movie, is a hoot. The top 25 entries are screened at the BFI, on the Southbank, in May.

> *Tickets on sale in December. BFI London Film Festival, page 142*

Bag a future masterpiece
London Art Fair

> londonartfair.co.uk

Witness one of London's more curious events
The Blessing of the River Thames

> cathedral.southwark.anglican.org

Now well into its fourth decade, the **London Art Fair** offers art lovers a great opportunity to see and buy international modern and contemporary work by both emerging and established artists. Usually in the third week of January, a hundred or so galleries set up stalls in the halls of the Business Design Centre in Islington, where with deep pockets it's possible to acquire works by the likes of Andy Warhol, David Hockney and Yinka Shonibare, as well as rub shoulders with emerging artists. It's an inclusive and accessible event, where you can often talk to gallerists and the artists themselves, or hear them speak at curated talks and panel discussions. Thanks to the fair's nurturing of talent and artists early in their career – Chris Ofili and Jenny Saville were both given 'rising star' awards at the 1996 edition – if you invest in a work you love, its value may well skyrocket over time.

One of London's quirkier happenings, **The Blessing of the River Thames** is a fairly recent celebration, dating from 2008. It takes place on a Sunday in mid-January on London Bridge. The congregations of Southwark Cathedral, on the south side, and St Magnus the Martyr, on the north meet in the middle, where a short ceremony is held after Choral Eucharist at Southwark Cathedral. Participants set off at 12.20 p.m. and the blessing occurs about ten minutes later, and is dedicated to those who work on and look after the River Thames. Special blessings are also said for those who have died in or near the river. The bells of St Magnus ring out, and a wooden cross is tossed into the water. The Blessing is a nod to the more Orthodox custom of hurling a cross into water as a symbol of Christ's baptism, celebrated on the Sunday after the Epiphany in countries such as Greece, Romania and Russia.

Get creative! It's time to enter the biggest open submission art show in the world

Royal Academy Summer Exhibition Call for Entries

> summer.royalacademy.org.uk

For more than two hundred and fifty years, each summer the Royal Academy of Arts been famously filling the halls of its prestigious Piccadilly gallery space with entries judged by a panel of Academicians – among them world famous artists such as Cornelia Parker, Anish Kapoor, Hew Locke, Sonia Boyce and Grayson Perry – who assess work sent in by thousands of amateur and professional artists. The first exhibition, in 1769, comprised 136 works by 56 artists, but these days some 1,600 works crowd every inch of wall space – and quite a lot of the floor, too. Complete unknowns sit cheek by jowl with art giants, and entry fees are reasonable (£40 per entry, with entries limited to two works). The submission window is open for around a month from the first week of January, but get work in early, as there's a cap of 16,500 submissions. Just want to see what the Academicians chose? See page 77.

> *Exhibition runs June-August*

Be brightened by a festival of light
Winter Lights

> canarywharf.com

A much-needed tonic, this festival of light illuminates the winter darkness with a mix of almost 20 temporary installations and permanent artworks. Installations are scattered across east London's Canary Wharf, and have included the mesmerising, flower-like *Neuron* by Spanish light artist Juan Fuentes (2024) – composed of thousands of luminous filaments – to the fun, immersive, walk-through experience of *Submergence* (2019, 2024) by the UK's Squidsoup. Many of the artworks hang over water, enhancing the experience even further, as in permanent piece *The Clew* by Portuguese Ottotto, which has 100 circles of bright red light encircling the Cubitt Steps Bridge. Held towards the end of January, and free throughout, the festival is open from 5–10 pm each night. It's busiest at weekends, so try to go during the week to get the most out of the displays. Around the same time, south of the river, a smaller set of light installations can be seen in and around Battersea Power Station in the Battersea Light Festival.

Celebrate Scotland's answer to the bard
Burns Night

> ceilidhclub.com

Quite why London goes to town on January 25 to celebrate the birth of Scotland's national poet Robert 'Rabbie' Burns (1759–96) remains something of a mystery, but go to town it does. Perhaps it's to do with the large Scots community living in the centre, perhaps it's because it's a lot of raucous fun. On and around **Burns Night**, readings of Burns' poems, traditional suppers of haggis, neeps and tatties, live music and ceilidhs with lots of dancing are just some of the many events that take place. Previous events have included a Burns Night ceilidh at Big Penny Social in Walthamstow, a traditional Scottish feast at the Ham Yard Hotel and an evening of live folk music aboard the *Cutty Sark* in Greenwich. If we had to recommend one event, however, it would be the Ceilidh Club's celebration at St Mary's Marylebone, where three hours of live music and Scottish dancing, well-priced food and drink, and, of course, the traditional Burns' 'Address to the Haggis', all guaranteeing a night of fun.

> *Tickets on sale in December*

Go *Galanthus* spotting
Snowdrop displays

> kew.org
> visitleevalley.org.uk

Snowdrops are one of the joys of the winter months, and they can be spotted from January through to March. Kew Gardens has the most varieties in London, found in the Rock Garden, the Alpine House and dotted around the woodland areas. They can be seen at Chelsea Physic Garden, where they're also for sale in the shop; it's a similar story at Myddelton House Gardens in Enfield, which holds an Ultimate Snowdrop Sale at the end of January, when local nurseries sell rarities alongside the more usual bulbs. Snowdrops are scattered on Hampstead Heath, particularly on the grassy verges near Kenwood House, and there's a lovely bank of them near the Albert Memorial in Kensington Gardens, not to mention a fine display along Central Avenue in Brompton Cemetery. Woodland areas are good hunting grounds, too – try heavily wooded Tower Hamlets Cemetery Park in Mile End, Oxleas Wood or Nunhead Cemetery in south-east London, Abney Park Cemetery in Stoke Newington or the arboretum at Morden Hall Park. More centrally, Bunhill Fields Burial Ground, just north of the City, has a host of early spring flowers, including snowdrops, scattered between the graves.

Fun for all the family at this annual cavalcade
London's New Year's Day Parade (LNYDP)

> lnydp.com

The **parade** is an annual extravaganza featuring 8,000 performers from all over the world, as well as community groups from 20 London boroughs – quite a leap from the 2,000 people who took part in the inaugural parade in 1987. The razzamatazz kicks off on Piccadilly, outside the Ritz hotel, at noon, and winds round Piccadilly Circus, past Trafalgar Square and down Whitehall to Westminster. It lasts about three hours. There are floats, double-decker buses and giant inflatables, interspersed with lots of marching bands, many from the United States, plus samba, steel and dhol bands (Indian drumming). Chinese dragons, circus artists, London's Pearly Kings and Queens and 200 or so Carnaval del Pueblo performers from across Latin America add to the impressive spectacle. There are motorbike stunts and a procession of Mini Moke cars, not to mention musical acts including Boyzlife and Chesney Hawkes. It's a family-friendly event, and perfect for anyone not spending the day in bed recovering from New Year's Eve celebrations.

Delight in the city's physical theatre and puppetry
MimeLondon

> mimelondon.com

MimeLondon emerged in 2024 in place of the London International Mime Festival (LIMF), the annual celebration of contemporary visual theatre which ran from 1977 to 2023. It's a scaled-back affair compared to LIMF at its peak, yet it continues to make an impact over the three weeks it runs, from late January to mid February. Here inventive productions are staged at such venues as the Barbican, the National Theatre, Sadlers Wells' Peacock Theatre and Shoreditch Town Hall. Participants in the inaugural season included physical theatre companies such as Gecko and Ockham's Razor, and French troupe Les Antliaclastes which staged Ambergris, a puppet operetta employing special effects, masks, marionettes and shadows.

Get lucky during London's winter shopping bonanza
January Sales

These days Boxing Day (26 December), or the day after, marks the start of the **January Sales** for big high-street names, with independent outlets often waiting for the New Year. Top-flight department stores are good hunting grounds for bargains: in London this means Harrods, Harvey Nichols, Selfridges and Liberty. The big shopping thoroughfares – Oxford Street, Regent Street, Brompton Road and King's Road – also reward eagle-eyed bargain hunters. Less frenetic search areas are neighbourhoods with a concentration of smaller boutiques, such as Covent Garden, Marylebone and Hampstead, while Bond Street is where to find a swathe of high-end shops. If the weather is winterly, try Westfield Stratford City in east London or Westfield London in Shepherd's Bush, west London.

Revel in ancient folklore on the South Bank
Twelfth Night

> thelionspart.co.uk

A good-natured (and free) celebration, **Twelfth Night** is organised by theatre troupe Lions Part. It takes place at the weekend on or after 6 January, outside Shakespeare's Globe on the Southbank. Festivities start with the Holly Man, the winter manifestation of the Green Man, dressed in green and adorned with foliage, being piped over the Thames, accompanied by Beelzebub. The Holly Man then wassails (toasts) the spectators, the Thames and the Globe, helped by the Bankside Mummers and the London Beadle.

The costumed Mummers then perform the traditional and boisterous St George Folk Combat Play on Bankside Jetty. At the end of the play, cakes are distributed; one contains a bean, another a pea, and the lucky recipients are hailed King and Queen for the day and crowned. The whole shebang, complete with crowd, then processes to Borough Yards for more dancing, storytelling and singing.

> *Lions Part sometimes also puts on an October Plenty performance, see page 139.*

Follow the dragon around Chinatown
Chinese New Year's Parade

> lccauk.com

Depending on the start of the lunar year, **Chinese New Year** falls either in late January or, more often, early to mid February. In 2025, the first new moon of the lunar year falls on 29 January, and marks the year of the snake, but in 2026 the date is 17 February (the year of the horse), and in 2027, 6 February (the turn of the goat). London sees the largest Chinese New Year celebrations outside Asia; the festivities are centred around Chinatown, buzzing with full-to-brimming restaurants and decked out for the occasion with vibrant red street decorations. The parade, held on the nearest Sunday to New Year, spills out into the surrounding streets, down Shaftesbury Avenue and along to Trafalgar Square. The procession, packed with floats and colourful dragon and lion dancers, is a crowdpleaser. There's also a family zone in Leicester Square, and food stalls and performance art in Trafalgar Square.

The Fierce Queens celebrate LGBTIA+
History Month at the National Maritime
Museum in Greenwich, page 24

February

Brighten up winter with some queer goings on
LGBTQIA+ History Month

> lgbtplushistorymonth.co.uk

This month-long celebration of queer history, achievements, knowledge, culture, and more, has been taking place across the UK every February since 2005, latterly under a themed banner which, in 2024, was medicine and healthcare. Event categories have ranged from exhibitions, comedy, cabaret and theatre to diverse talks, workshops and tutorials, both live and online. Meet-ups form a big part of the month, with eat-outs, pub nights, walking tours, catch-ups and film nights offering the chance to discuss everything from parenting to local LGBTQIA+ history. Around the city many public spaces and galleries curate whole programmes – Bermondsey Project Space, Tate Modern, the British Library and Greenwich's National Maritime Museum are just a few that have put on great events in recent years, among them Tall Child (pictured) performing as part of a Queer Noise event at Bermondsey Project Space. The home website lists all events, with some bookable a couple of months in advance – and it's worth noting that many take place in January.

> *Tickets on sale in November*

Turn your church frown upside down
Clown's Service

> trinitysaintsunited.co.uk/clown-service

This odd but uplifting event has its roots back in 1946, when, as a publicity stunt, circus owner Billy Smart arranged for his clowns to lay a wreath on the gravestone of father of clowns Joseph Grimaldi, then located in the graveyard of St James's, Pentonville. Thus was born an annual tradition which eventually expanded into a church service, now held each year in the east London church of All Saints in Haggerston. Taking place on the first Sunday of February, the **Clown's Service** is an exuberant affair filled with colourful clowns, held at a time when mental health is often at its lowest. So, it's open to everyone, and it is as much a celebration of joy, laughter and creativity as it is remembering Grimaldi. Expect clowns dressed in their finest outfits, complete with buttonholes that spray water, and readings accompanied by balloon animals in a surreal, fun-filled event, with a clown show and generous supply of clown cake after the service. At other times of the year, you can pay your own personal tribute to Grimaldi in Islington's Joseph Grimaldi Park. If you happen to be there on 31 May, the anniversary of Grimaldi's death, you'll almost certainly encounter a clown or two paying tribute. Don't be surprised if you see them literally dancing on his grave while one of the two coffin-shaped metal memorials sings back!

Toss crepes in the City
Pancake Day Races

> lambtavernleadenhall.com

Is there a more surreal sight than City types in starched shirts and pressed suits racing through the cobbled stones of Leadenhall market flipping pancakes as though their annual bonus depended on it? That's just one of the many pancake races held in the capital on Shrove Tuesday. While watching them is fun, participating in them is even more so – though you'll want to practise your tossing on the move as most require at least one flip during the race. Unsurprisingly spaces on the Leadenhall one, organised by the nearby Lamb Tavern, go fast, so register your team of up to four people well in advance and who knows, your name could end up engraved on the legendary golden frying pan trophy for the year. Just want to watch? The pub usually gives away free pancakes to spectators on a first-come, first-served basis, so get there early for the fun, which usually begins at 1 p.m. Another standout race to watch is the Inter Livery Pancake Race at Guildhall Yard, where participants dress in ceremonial robes topped with colourful chef's hats.

Admire sporting prowess at its most noble
Six Nations Rugby Union

> sixnationsrugby.com

These days it's debatable that the six national teams involved in this annual competition – England, Ireland, Scotland, Wales, France and Italy – are anywhere near the world's best, but the passion felt by their fans, and the bonhomie they exude as they watch their teams play each other in a tournament whose first iteration began in 1883, is still as strong as it ever was. The sporting courage (aka insanity) and nobility is a pleasure to witness live at England's home ground of Twickenham, but if you don't have a ticket, which are as rare as hens' teeth, hundreds of pubs in London show the games in convivial evenings filled with song (banners outside usually indicate the best ones to see them in). The action begins on the first weekend in February and culminates on the second or third Saturday in March; to find out when and how tickets go on sale, sign up to the Union mailing list.

Meet the authors at the long-running Jewish Literary Foundation's literary fair
Book Week

> jewishliteraryfoundation.co.uk

Book Week, formerly known as Jewish Book Week, was renamed in 2024. Presented by the Jewish Literary Foundation, it started as a small, four-day event in 1952 and is now a mighty ten-day juggernaut taking place in late February/early March, and is London's longest-running literary festival. The varied content is spread across multiple genres, from graphic novels and music criticism to history and memoir, and encompasses readings, performances, lectures and discussions. Events are held at the multi-platform arts space Kings Place, and online; many are free. Over the years, plenty of well-known names have headlined, including Janet Suzman, Jonathan Freedland and Simon Schama. 2024 saw 90 events, running from a discussion on 'Being Jewish in Modern Britain' chaired by Hugo Rifkind to a celebration of Leonard Bernstein (with live music), and from Daniel Finkelstein discussing his bestseller *Hitler, Stalin, Mum & Dad* to Silvia Nacamulli talking about her cookbook *Jewish Flavours of Italy*; Simon Schama was the keynote speaker. The Jewish Literary Foundation also provides an 'Authors in Schools' programme.

> *Tickets on sale in December*

Bask in a blast of exotically coloured flowers
Kew Orchid Festival

> kew.org

The Royal Botanical Gardens at Kew's annual **Orchid Festival** runs from early February to early March, and injects a welcome shot of colour into what are often grey months. Orchids are one of the world's most successful plant families; they are found on almost every continent, and each year the Richmond-based garden focuses on a different country. It was Cameroon's turn in 2023, when Kew highlighted how endangered some of the country's amazing specimens are, while in 2024 the centre of attention was biodiverse Madagascar, with the garden's Malagasy orchids showcased alongside varieties from all over the world. The orchids are on display in the tropical Princess of Wales conservatory, some forming living sculptures, though others can be found in the Palm and Temperate Houses, and hardy species in the Rock Garden and wildflower areas. Entrance to the Orchid Festival is included with the entrance fee to Kew Gardens. On Fridays and Saturdays there are also ticketed evening events with themed music, talks, food and drinks.

Get involved in this joyful kids' celebration
Imagine Children's Festival

> southbankcentre.co.uk

FEB

Spread over 11 days in early February, this vibrant **children's festival** enlivens the Southbank Centre, with a variety of performances and activities designed to appeal to all kinds of kids, whatever their interests or capabilities. It features theatre, comedy, puppetry, dance, storytelling, installation, creative art spaces and more, offering an eclectic roster of performers, from children's authors such as John Agard and Michael Rosen to the David Gibb Big Band. Previous years have seen day-long events like ZooNation's Hip-Hop Half Term – a blend of workshops, a DJ jam and a performance from ZooNation's Youth Company – and targeted performances such as *The River*, Bamboozle Theatre Company's show for disabled children with complex needs. Almost half the events are free and many of them interactive. Imagine aims to be inclusive and welcoming to all. A relaxed policy means visitors can enter and leave events freely and there is an open attitude towards audience noise.

Holi festival celebrations at Battersea
Power Station, page 43

March

See the C&W stars shine
Country to Country Festival

> c2c-countrytocountry.com

Over three days in early March, the biggest country festival in Europe, **Country to Country**, attracts some of the best US acts to London's O2 arena. In 2024, the headliners were chart-topper Kane Brown, plus returning acts Brad Paisley, multi-award winner and member of the Grand Ole Opry, and popular modern-country band Old Dominion. It also featured Nashville favourite singer–songwriter Conner Smith, and bestselling sibling duo the Brothers Osborne. The Spotlight Stage showcased up-and-comers such as Mexican-Oklahoman Wyatt Flores, and crossover artists like Lily Rose and Fancy Hagood. The first C2C was staged in 2013; it was a smaller event, but had an impressive line-up – headlining Carrie Underwood and Tim McGraw. BBC Radio 2 broadcasts the event, 2024 marking veteran presenter and country aficionado Bob Harris's tenth stint as host.

> *Tickets on sale in October*

Witness a closely fought skirmish on the Thames
Head of the River Race

> horr.co.uk

A hotly contested men's event, the **Head of the River Race** runs 4.25 miles from Mortlake to Putney (the reverse of the annual Boat Race) and features open eights. It was founded in 1926 by rowing coach Steve Fairbairn, to give crews an incentive after winter training. A maximum of 400 boats can compete, and within that, up to 60 overseas crews are permitted. In any year, there are usually well over 300 eights on the water. Various trophies are awarded alongside the winner's prize, the Fairbairn; they include the fastest university or college team, the Bernard Churcher; and fastest overseas crew and fastest junior crew. Oxford Brookes University Boat Club (crew A) won the Fairbairn in 2023 and set a new course record of 16 minutes 28.04 seconds in the process. The race takes place on a Saturday in late March, with the start time (morning or afternoon) decided by the tide. Crews set off at 10-second intervals, so the whole event takes about two hours – plenty of time to soak up the excitement from the riverbank.

> *Entries open early January–mid-February*

Experience an explosion of pink
Cherry Blossom

> london.gov.uk

London is blessed with an abundance of blossom, though some areas look more spring-like than others. Barnes, for example, has street after street lined with flowering trees, as do the residential areas of Kensington. Across the city, there's a glorious collection of cherry trees on Aldgate Square. Some parks are inevitably more colourful than others. It's no surprise that the Royal Botantical Gardens at Kew has a great variety of cherry trees which bloom from late March to the beginning of May. Look for the spectacular Cherry Walk, behind the Palm House. In the south of the city, Greenwich Park also has a beautiful stretch of cherry trees near the Rose Garden, and there's good **cherry blossom** to be had in the more centrally based Kensington Gardens (near the Albert Memorial) and Regent's Park (in the Avenue Garden). A more recent addition is the London Blossom Garden in the Queen Elizabeth Olympic Park, E20, near the Timber Lodge Café. Opened on 24 May 2021, the garden is a living memorial to those who lost their lives in the coronavirus pandemic. It holds 33 trees, one for each London borough, and crab apple, plum and hawthorn trees sit alongside the cherry trees.

Wander through endless yellow with a spring flower walk

Daffodil Walks

> mariecurie.org.uk

Does anything mark the arrival of spring with more gaudy exuberance than parks, riverbanks and woodlands awash with **daffodils**? From tiny delicate varieties to the bright Jaffa cake orange of larger cultivated blooms, London is filled with narcissi from as early as February, but March is really daffodil month here, when many otherwise bare parks are blanketed in gold. In flowerbed-free Royal Green Park, they're the only flowers you'll see, while at Hampton Court's Wilderness Garden, a range of varieties are joined by winter jasmine and forget-me-nots. On the banks surrounding Hyde Park's Serpentine, opposite Buckingham Palace and to the south side of The Mall in St James's Park, crowding the beds of Victoria Embankment Gardens and Kew Gardens and all over Golders Hill Park, you'll find equally splendid shows. For a different daffodil vibe, London's garden cemeteries, many nature conservation sites, spring into colour in February blooming on into March, with clusters of daffodils and snowdrops, crocuses and hyacinths offering these lovely green spaces an added layer of beauty and pathos. And not to be forgotten, the banks of the River Thames offer wonderful daffodil walks, notably in Richmond. Daffodils, with their bright, cheery beauty, have become the symbol of hope for many cancer charities: Marie Curie runs the Great Daffodil Appeal in March.

Get some tips on how to achieve domestic bliss
Ideal Home Show

> idealhomeshow.co.uk

Established in 1908, the **Ideal Home Show** nowadays encompasses all things domestic. It takes place in late March and early April, and is based at London's Olympia. The centrepiece is the annual show home (the Dream Home), with 2024 demonstrating the largest, most lavish event yet. Hundreds of exhibitors, running from companies specialising in everything from sliding doors and fold-up beds to furniture and gifts, turn up. And it's not just all fixtures, fittings and home decor: new technology, feng shui, garden trends and energy saving innovations, among others, are also covered. In addition there are bookable, craft-focused workshops (wreath-making, upcycling), an advice hub and talks by celebrity experts such as Martin Lewis and George Clarke. The Eat & Drink element includes tips from well-known practitioners, food from across the globe, mixology sessions and, of course, the chance to shop (and sample) in the Artisan Producers Market.

Bag some art without breaking the bank
Affordable Art Fair

> affordableartfair.com

There is genuinely something for everyone at the tri-annual Affordable Art Fair, both in terms of tastes and pocket depths. More than a hundred galleries and artists converge on Battersea Park in spring and autumn (March and October), and Hampstead Heath in spring (usually early May), to sell thousands of original artworks in all their myriad forms. The breadth of work on offer virtually guarantees you'll fall in love with something, whether it's a limited-edition linocut print of the sun setting on London's skyline, drawings or paintings created using every kind of medium available. Prices range from a very affordable £50 to £7,500, and the settings of Battersea Park and Hampstead Heath turn a visit to a gallery into a grand day out, with the opportunity to admire your purchases over a cuppa or a glass of something at one of the bars and cafés there. Check out the website to see other Affordable Art Fairs globally, too.

> For London Art Fair, see page 14

Cheer on the Blues
Oxford–Cambridge University Boat Race

> theboatrace.org

The last Saturday of March sees thousands of landlubbers mass on the 4-mile stretch of the Thames between Putney Bridge and Chiswick Bridge to watch teams of eight rowers, plus their coxes, all Oxford and Cambridge University students, give it their all in the Men's Boat Race. Racing upstream on the incoming "flood" tide and clad in duck egg blue (Cambridge) or dark blue (Oxford), the crews set off from the University Stone, set into the towpath on Putney Embankment, 90 minutes before high tide, with the women's race held an hour before the men's, so that crews are rowing with the fastest possible current. The speed, synergy and grace the rowers achieve is unparalleled, particularly as they take the Surrey bend under Hammersmith Bridge. Eighty percent of crews leading at this point go on to win the race, and it's a great spot from which to watch events unfold; but really, just being anywhere along the route, or in one of the two fan parks, make it one of London's most memorable free events.

Celebrate Queer cinema in the capital
BFI Flare LGBTQIA+ Film Festival
> player.bfi.org.uk

Browse a curated selection of homewares
Midcentury Modern Shows
> modernshows.com

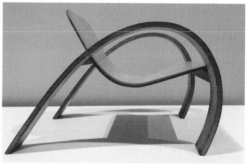

Each spring, Britain's most prestigious film organisation puts on this celebration of queer cinema, live at the BFI Southbank and streamed through BFI Player. Drawing on movies from around the globe, the programme mines established and emerging talent, and offers a rare opportunity to experience diverse voices from vastly differing cultures and communities from as far afield as Guyana, Northern Ireland, Cyprus, Nigeria and South Korea, among others. Each screening brings together a lively mix of experiences, such as a 12-minute experimental drama from Jamaica about a genderqueer person and a full-length Sundance-award winning narrative drama from Finnish director Alli Haapasalo. The screenings are bolstered by a range of events and archive titles, with curated mini-programmes by top film critics like Mark Kermode and screen talks by the likes of Elliot Page (pictured).

What started on a small scale in 2002, when Petra Curtis and Lucy Ryder Richardson held a home-based sale, has grown to become a destination furniture and home accessories fair. Held twice a year, in March and November, usually at Dulwich College, in south London, **Midcentury Modern** is a showcase for some of the best independent mid-century dealers, as well as a scattering of contemporary designers. There are 85 stalls and it's all quality stuff, so whatever you're interested in, you'll doubtless find a stallholder with a similar passion: studio pottery, Scandinavian glass, leather sofas, 1960s lamps and any amount of teak furniture are sold alongside classic posters and other ephemera. Rare and immaculate pieces cost a lot of money, but there are plenty of items priced at impulse-buy level, and the browsing is fun, even if all you leave with is a coffee and a stylish birthday card.

Salute women past and present
Women's History Month

> womenshistorymonth.gov

Built in March around the annual International Women's Day on 8 March, **Women's History Month** is a recognition of women's and trans women's contributions to arts, history, culture, society and technology. It takes its cue from the US, where it's been observed annually since 1987. Many of London's galleries, theatres, museums and other cultural or educational spaces put on special events throughout the month, from talks and tours to live performance and art workshops. Past events have included a live online tour exploring paintings representing women at the National Gallery, painting workshops and comedy evenings at the Royal Museums Greenwich. In 2023, Battersea Power Station got in on the act with a Prince's Trust International Women's Day Marketplace, and the nearby Affordable Art Fair, in Battersea Park, featured an exhibition of living women and female-identifying artists. Yet it's not just about culture: women, non-binary people and their allies take part in a group hour-long bike ride around central London landmarks, as a celebration of WHM and in a call for safe cycling for everyone, led by the London Cycling Campaign.

> For Affordable Art Fair, see page 38

Cultural Festivals

The eclectic festivals that run throughout the year play a big part in making the city such a cultural powerhouse. The depth and variety of what's on offer is thrilling, covering opera, literature, music, art and comedy, and featuring everything from family activities to baton-twirling processions, sacred rites to community get-togethers. Festivals add another dimension to city life, and offer a glimpse of hitherto hidden corners of London.

BFI Future Film Festival

> Southbank; bfi.org.uk; mid-February

A four-day festival for aspiring filmmakers aged 16–25, held at BFI Southbank, in cinemas across the UK, and online. Events in London include screenings, masterclasses and workshops, with opportunities for networking.

St Patrick's Day Parade and Festival

> Trafalgar Square; london.gov.uk;
>   Sunday close to 17 March

A celebration of all things Irish, held over a Sunday afternoon in central London. The procession, featuring marching bands and dancers, winds its way from Hyde Park Corner to Trafalgar Square, where family friendly entertainment includes the best of Irish food and arts - concerts, choirs, film and dancing.

Kinoteka Polish Film Festival

> Across London; kinoteka.org.uk; March

Held over three weeks, this long-running event (2025 marks its 23rd year) showcases a diverse range of Polish films. Organised by the Polish Cultural Institute, and supported by the Polish Film Institute, it has several strands, including New Polish Cinema, Documentaries and Polish Cinema Classics. Among the featured venues are: the BFI Southbank, ICA, Ognisko Polskie, Prince Charles Cinema and POSK (Polish Social & Cultural Association).

Vaisakhi

> Trafalgar Square; london.gov.uk;
>   Saturday in early April

Vaisakhi is a celebration of Sikh and Punjabi culture and marks the birth of modern-day Sikhism. Musicians, dance troupes and food stalls take over Trafalgar Square for the afternoon, and there are also talks and martial arts' demonstrations.

Holi

> Across London; timeout.com; March

The centuries-old Hindu festival Holi is also known as the Festival of Colours, an indication of its vibrant and joyful nature. Paint fights, involving vividly coloured powder paints, are the most eye-catching aspect, but food and music also feature, making for a joyous occasion. Most boroughs in London have events.

Horniman Spring Fair

> Forest Hill; horniman.ac.uk;
>   Saturday in March/April

Held in the gardens of the Horniman Museum, the Spring Fair is a family-focused event, with food stalls, party games, a singalong, a disco, giant bubbles, fun workshops and an Easter bonnet parade. There also are opportunities to see the resident animals – alpacas, goats and rabbits.

Crystal Palace Festival

> Crystal Palace; crystalpalacefestival.org;
>   weekend in mid-September

A community-focused arts and culture festival, first seen in 2011, which takes place in Crystal Palace park and at venues dotted around the Crystal Palace Triangle. Events include everything from DJ sets and musical performances, featuring local choirs and bands, through to an arts and crafts tent and child-friendly workshops and dance sessions.

Carnaval Del Pueblo

> Burgess Park; carnavaldelpueblo.co.uk;
>   Sunday in August

The largest Latin American carnival in Europe has it all – music, dancing, extravagant costumes and lots of food. From noon, a procession wends its way from Potters Fields Park, near Tower Bridge, to Burgess Park, where the rest of the festival takes place. As well as food stalls, there are children's activities, and musicians play from 3 p.m., across several stages.

London Games Festival

> Across London; games.london; April

A festival devoted to video games and interactive entertainment, held at various venues across the capital over several weeks. Some events are ticketed, some free. Highlights are the BAFTA Game Awards and Now Play This, a mini festival of independent and innovative games from all over the world, held at Somerset House.

Open City Documentary Festival

> Across London; opencitylondon.com; week in April

A celebration of non-fiction cinema featuring work by emerging directors and retrospectives of older, often little-seen works. As well as screenings, there are talks and workshops. Venues include Rich Mix, ICA, Curzon Soho and Barbican.

In a Field by a Bridge Festival

> Tower Bridge; inafieldbyabridge.com;
> weekend in July

This 'celebration of low-impact living and community action' focusing on the London Bridge Area is held in Potters Field Park and St John's Churchyard, right by Tower Bridge. Music, entertainment, food, stalls and workshops all feature in the two-day event, which is free to attend.

Camden Fringe

> Camden; camdenfringe.com;
> late July to late August

There's a dizzying choice of events spread over a range of venues at this performing arts festival. Stand-up and improv comedy, spoken word, theatre, opera, dance, musicals and children's shows have all featured. What's more, prices are affordable, and shows short and sweet (around an hour).

Battersea Games

> Battersea Power Station;
> batterseapowerstation.co.uk; July to September

Battersea Power Station hosts a range of free and ticketed sports and games, involving a running track, a padel court and a mini basketball court, plus a dedicated area for fitness classes and a climbing wall. Dogs can get a workout too, with an agility course and training sessions by Battersea Dogs and Cats Home.

Bloomsbury Festival

> Bloomsbury; bloomsburyfestival.org.uk;
> ten days in October

There's something for everyone at the Bloomsbury Festival, as the programme includes hundreds of events across art, music, theatre and science. There are walks, talks and demonstrations. Venues include the Crypt Gallery at St Pancras Church, Conway Hall, Brunswick Square and Holborn Library.

Procession of Our Lady of Mount Carmel

> Clerkenwell; italianchurch.org.uk;
Saturday in July

Nobody seems sure exactly when this Italian community tradition started, but it was sometime in the 1880s, and now, on a Saturday in July, head to Clerkenwell Road, where the statue of Our Lady of Mount Carmel is carried around the area surrounding St Peter's Italian church. Come to watch the procession, admire the floats and banners and, afterwards, enjoy the Italian food stalls in nearby Warner Street.

Woolwich Contemporary Print Fair (WCPF)

> Royal Arsenal, Woolwich; woolwichprintfair.com;
four days in late November

The WCPF showcases more than a thousand artworks, across many styles and techniques, from famous names to unknowns. The Fair was started in 2016 in order to give a platform to emerging artists and to democratise the collecting process, as well as help explain printmaking processes and techniques. There are printing demonstations and talks, and evening social events.

MCM Comic Con

> ExCeL London; mcmcomiccon.com; May

A jamboree of all things anime, TV and film, held over three days. There are signings, panel discussions, celebrity Q&As, cosplay and other competitions, screenings, gaming, workshops and kids' activities, not to mention plenty of merch opportunities.

Chiswick Book Festival

> Chiswick; chiswickbookfestival.net;
> week in September

Held in various venues across Chiswick, this book festival covers everything from poetry and biography to children's literature and cookery books. It attracts some big names, too – past speakers have included Jacqueline Wilson, Clive Myrie and Michael Frayn.

Queen's Park Book festival

> Queen's Park; queensparkbookfestival.co.uk;
> weekend in September

A literary book festival with an impressive roster of past guests: Zadie Smith, Tessa Hadley, Robert Harris and Bernardine Evaristo have all spoken here. The event also has a Community Tent, where local voices and under-represented groups are championed.

Greenwich Comedy Festival

> National Maritime Museum;
> greenwichcomedyfestival.co.uk;
> week in September

Billed as London's biggest 'comedy spectacular', this open-air festival has craft beer and street food alongside well-known comics and rising talent. Jack Dee, Fern Brady, Phil Wang, Brett Goldstein and Sindhu Vee are just some of the performers from the last few years.

Chelsea History Festival

> Chelsea; chelseahistoryfestival.com;
> last week in September

Run by and located in the National Army Museum, the Royal Hospital Chelsea and Chelsea Physic Garden, the Chelsea History Festival was founded in 2019. The aim is to 'entertain, educate and inspire', via local and world history, by way of talks, tours, films and family activities. Previous historians and celebrities include Alison Weir, Helen Fry, Michael Palin and Bill Wyman.

London Photo Show

> Bargehouse Gallery, Southbank;
> londonphotoshow.org; four days in November

Photographers from all over the world, and from all kinds of backgrounds, submit their work for inclusion in this group show – meaning that the public get to see (and buy) a truly eclectic mix of art.

Feria de Londres

> Wembley Park; wembleypark.com;
> weekend in late July

Billed as London's biggest festival of Spanish culture, the Feria de Londres features everything from Spanish food and drink stalls to dancing workshops. Enjoy free entertainment and music stages, as well as ticketed events in the evening.

Diwali

> Trafalgar Square; london.gov.uk;
  October or November

Diwali, known as the festival of lights, is important to Hindus, Sikhs, Jains and Buddhists and is normally celebrated in October or November. There are a variety of events across London (many restaurants and some museums mark the festival), but the biggest celebration is held in Trafalgar Square on a Sunday near Diwali, with music, dancing, activities and food. All are welcome.

April

Enjoy the spring fields of blue
Bluebell Walks

Get up early for this Easter tradition
St Bride's Egg-Rolling

> stbrides.com

If the winter has been mild, then **bluebells** may start to appear in late March, but you're guaranteed to see them in April. Central London parks have scattered batches of bluebells, but head beyond zones 1 and 2 to see them in all their glory. Anywhere with woodland is worth checking out: in north London, Bluebell Wood is a remnant of an ancient wood, tucked away next to Muswell Hill Golf Club; Highgate Wood and Kenwood House also have drifts of bluebells. Moving east, Epping Forest, Tower Hamlets Cemetery and Wanstead Park are good bets; in the south-west, Isabella Plantation (better known for azaleas and rhododendrons), has a good showing, as do Beckenham Place Park and Oxleas Wood in the south-east. In west London, Kew has bluebells in the natural area near Queen Charlotte's Cottage, while Osterley Park is worth a visit too.

Be prepared to get up early to experience this London tradition at beautiful St Bride's church in the City of London, designed by Christopher Wren. The **egg-rolling** fun starts after the 6 a.m. Communion service on Easter Sunday. Everyone is welcome, but people are asked to bring their own hard-boiled eggs, preferably decorated ones. The congregation walks the short distance from the church to Fleet Street, where people take turns to roll hard-boiled eggs down the road – there's a prize (chocolate) for the person who rolls their unbroken egg the furthest. Afterwards breakfast is offered back at St Bride's. The egg-rolling apparently symbolises new life and the stone being rolled from Christ's tomb.

Treat Easter as a chocolate-fest
Egg Hunts

Easter also has a more self-indulgent side, best represented by the **Easter egg hunts** found around the capital. Hampton Court Palace holds a family-focused Lindt Gold Bunny Hunt over several weeks around Easter, and several National Trust properties have egg trails, notably Ham House and Sutton House. However, if you want to see the most decadent, highly decorated chocolate eggs of all, take a trip to the food halls at Fortnum & Mason or Harrods.

Enjoy a family-friendly festival of Englishness
The Feast of St George

> london.gov.uk

Celebrate the Easter holiday with magnificent music
Easter Music

A family-friendly day festival staged by the Mayor of London in honour of England's patron saint, the **Feast of St George** celebrates its twentieth year in 2027. The fun takes place in Trafalgar Square, on a Sunday afternoon on or around 23 April, St George's Day, and aims to celebrate Englishness in all its diverse forms. As well as a roster of acts – everything from individual performers to choirs – there are market stalls, food concessions and family-focused games and activities. Legend has it that St George slayed a terrifying dragon, so expect beasts, in whatever form, to make an appearance.

Certain London events are synonymous with Easter – for example, it's a great time to catch a performance of Handel's *Messiah* in splendid surroundings. The Royal Albert Hall has staged the Royal Choral Society's *Messiah* every Good Friday afternoon since 1876, with gaps for catastrophic events – the Blitz in 1940–41 and the global pandemic of 2020–21. Cadogan Hall, in Bloomsbury, usually puts on a performance around Easter, as do many of London's churches.

Admire some of the showiest plants in London
Azalea and Rhododendron Spotting

> royalparks.org.uk

APR

The best-known place to see azaleas and rhododendrons in London is the Isabella Plantation – and deservedly so. It's a lovely 40-acre woodland garden set within Richmond Park and holds the National Plant Collection of Wilson 50 Kurume Azaleas, which plant collector Ernest Wilson first brought over from Japan in the 1920s, plus many rhododendron, magnolia and camellia shrubs. Over in south London's Dulwich Park, the American Garden has masses of azaleas and rhododendrons planted around lawns, while in the north's Kenwood House, the Humphry Repton-designed garden is packed with dense banks of different rhododendrons. Naturally, Kew, in the west, has some hybrids not found elsewhere, but the real reason to come is to see the dramatic effect of the Rhododendron Dell at its peak. In London, April and May are the best months to see azaleas and rhododendrons in full, glorious bloom.

Bicycling in style
Tweed Run

> tweedrun.com

Established in 2009, when around 300 riders took part, the **Tweed Run** is a self-described 'metropolitan bicycle ride with a bit of style'. Held on a Saturday in late April, the ride is ticketed and up to 1,000 tickets go on sale in mid-March and sell out quickly. The run includes a tea break and a picnic stop with entertainment, plus some guaranteed revelry after it's over for those who've taken part. Dressing up is a must. As the name suggests, many cyclists turn up wearing tweed – plus fours are a popular choice – and some riders have vintage bicycles or tandems. The exact route is kept secret until just before the day, but it always runs through central London. Previous starting points have included Clerkenwell, Somerset House and St Paul's Cathedral. At the finish, there are cocktails, and prizes are awarded in various categories, including Best Dressed (Man, Woman or Bicycle) and Best Moustache. A tip from the etiquette section of the website: bowler hats are 'a spot' more aerodynamic than top hats!

> *Tickets on sale in mid-March*

See the making of champions
The TCS London Marathon & Mini London Marathon Ballot

> tcslondonmarathon.com

The biggest event in the UK runner's calendar attracts hundreds of thousands of entries to its annual ballot for places – indeed last year's numbers made history with more than half a million applications. Around 10 per cent of them get a space in the race. If you want to be one of them, read on. **The London Marathon** Ballot opens for just one week each April, for entry in the following year's race. Successful entrants are notified by July, and have until 1 August to pay their entry fee. If you're really dead-set on getting a spot, donate your entry fee to the London Marathon Foundation when you enter the ballot and you'll automatically be entered into a second ballot, doubling your chances of getting a place – plus you pay a reduced entry fee if you're successful in either ballot. And if you're unsuccessful in both, you get a smart winter training top as consolation. Charity places are also a good way of trying to get a place – the website lists all the charities you can apply through, with details and links.

Cheer on the world's best runners
TCS London Marathon & Mini London Marathon

> tcslondonmarathon.com

Whether you're an unsuccessful participant, a would-be runner or cheering on loved ones, as a spectator to the **London Marathon**, the biggest event in the UK runners' calendar, you can watch around 50,000 people tackle the 26.2-mile route from Greenwich Park, in the south, to the Mall in central London. Popular vantage points such as Tower Bridge get rammed, but other spots such as Canada Water will afford you a front-row view of the action at a point where the runners are still in pretty great shape. That said, support at Canary Wharf is a huge motivational force for those feeling the burn after 18 miles of slog. And when it's all over, want to party? Get yourself over to Limehouse, where the Run Dem Crew, formed by DJ, poet and writer Charlie Dark, have turned the Marathon into a kind of mini Notting Hill Carnival, albeit in east rather than west London. And if your little ones are keen on entering the fun (and receiving their own medal after crossing the iconic finish line), get their school to enter the TCS Mini London Marathon. Children and young people can run, jog, walk or wheel 1 mile (Reception to Year 7) or 2.6 miles (Years 4–12) in the heart of the capital. Events for young and old, alike.

Be moved by a mesmerising Easter performance
Wintershall Passion of Jesus

> wintershall.org.uk

APR

Trafalgar Square hosts many events and gatherings over the year, but perhaps none quite as strange as the **Wintershall Passion of Jesus**, a darkly realistic interpretation of the crucifixion that is as unsettling as it is unusual. Its roots lie in 1989, when Ann and Peter Hutley (also the writer) began holding open-air performances about the life of Jesus at their 1,000-acre estate, Wintershall in Surrey. From a small-scale interpretation of the nativity via the commissioning over 20 years of the stations of the cross (in materials including bronze, timber, steel and marble), the Hutleys arrived at the apotheosis of their calendar year in the heart of London, where more than a hundred costumed Wintershall players, as well as donkeys, horses and doves, bring their electric and moving portrayal of the final days of Jesus to the capital's most iconic space. Two performances, at 12 noon and 3:15 p.m., are free, though anyone wanting to reserve a space in the small Designated Accessibility Area will need to book a few months before the event (February, at time of writing). The performances are projected onto a screen and BSL-interpreted so that the multi-faith thousands who gather can enjoy the experience.

Fancy a free hot cross bun at London's oldest surviving church?
The London Butterworth Charity and Widow's Sixpence

> greatstbarts.com

There are many reasons to visit the stunning Smithfields-based Priory Church of St Bartholomew the Great, as its weekly hour-long tours reveal. Highlights of the just over 900-year-old building, the oldest parish church in London, include a chapel that was once the printshop where Benjamin Franklin - yes, *that* Benjamin Franklin - was apprenticed in 1724. The artist William Hogarth was christened in the church font and there's even a tomb that weeps. The surroundings are so beautiful they've featured in many a film, including *Four Weddings and a Funeral* and *Shakespeare in Love*. But if that's not enough to draw you in, on Good Friday, each year, there's an added incentive of free, buttered hot cross buns as part of a Good Friday practice that dates back to the nineteenth century. **The London Butterworth Charity and Widow's Sixpence** references a custom of Victorian gentlemen handing out a sixpence and a bun to impoverished widows in the parish, from funds provided by publisher Joshua Butterworth, while standing atop a table tomb in the church's graveyard. These days, the rector offers money - 20 shillings - from his position at the same tomb, a sermon is accompanied by hymns, and hot cross buns are doled out to everyone present. A lovely, centuries-old London tradition.

The wonder of wisteria hysteria
Wisteria Walks

There's perhaps no one plant that shows off the Georgian, Victorian and Edwardian architecture of London's more prosperous neighbourhoods better than wisteria. Its elegant purple – and, increasingly white, pink, and blue – candle flowers draping and creeping over bright wedding-cake white townhouse fronts and wrought iron railings are a sight to behold across the capital. Wander around the streets of Chelsea, Chiswick, Notting Hill, Hampstead and Kensington, in particular, in late spring and you'll find plenty of Instagrammable spots in streets and parks - including Fulham Palace, Holland Park and Chelsea Physic Garden – but London is also home to gorgeous wisteria displays across its wider boroughs too. In Battersea Park, the rejuvenated Old English Garden is the place to head, while Peckham Rye Park's Sexby Garden offers a gorgeous tunnel of purple, which, arguably, offers the most perfect wisteria photo op in the city. Further afield, Hillingdon is home to the Eastcote House Gardens, which, again, offers a lovely display.

May

Enjoy classy music in an unstuffy setting
Opera Holland Park

> operahollandpark.com

A truly ancient Tower of London custom
Beating the Bounds

> ahbtt.org.uk; hrp.org.uk

A three-month summer festival, **Opera Holland Park** runs from late May to early August, and is held in a canopied open-air auditorium in the park. There's something for everyone: a Gilbert & Sullivan comedy (in 2024 it was *A Yeoman of the Guard*) to less-often performed pieces such as Handel's *Acis and Galatea*, as well as classics such as Puccini's *Tosca*, Rossini's *The Barber of Seville* or Bizet's *Carmen* (pictured). The opera company was founded in 1996, and the City of London Sinfonia has been the resident orchestra since 2003. There is no dress code – organisers are keen to encourage attendance by people who haven't seen opera before – though layers are advisable to cope with the vagaries of the English summer. Unless you're a member, ticket sales open in early March.

An ancient English custom, **Beating the Bounds** dates from the Middle Ages, when parish boundaries would be reaffirmed by the act of processing around them and stopping to beat each boundary marker. In London, the church of All Hallows by the Tower observes this tradition on Ascension Day. A party including clergy, officials from associated Livery Companies (in full regalia) and children from St Dunstan's College in Catford leaves the church at 4.15 p.m. and returns in time for evensong at 6 p.m. It takes that long because the south boundary is in the middle of the Thames, and so a boat is involved. Every third year (and 2025 is one of those years) there's a pretend battle with the Yeoman Warders of the Tower of London at the shared boundary mark – a marker that was always in dispute (in 1698 there was even a riot).

> *Tickets on sale in early March*

Marvel at the brightly decorated canal boats
Canalway Cavalcade

> waterways.org.uk

The **Canalway Cavalcade** in affluent Little Venice, has been going for more than 40 years and is held over the first bank holiday in May. It's a celebration of the life and community on London's waterways, at the junction where the Grand Union Canal and Regents Canal meet, and is organised by the Inland Waterways Association, a charity dedicated to supporting and regenerating Britain's canals and rivers. Visitors can attend by boat (you must book a mooring) or on foot, and the event attracts thousands of people. The cavalcade is a family-friendly event, at which over 100 boats line the canal and pack into the Pool at Little Venice, including narrowboats, barges and cruisers, all hoping to win the prize for Best Decorated Boat. Rembrandt Gardens, overlooking the canal, is the venue for much of the entertainment, from face-painting for kids to a Friday night quiz and a Saturday night variety show for adults. There are also craft stalls, children's entertainment, live music and refreshments, including a real ale bar, alongside the brightly coloured boats. Stay till dark on Sunday to catch the Procession of Illuminated Boats: the display is quite something.

Revel in Chelsea colours
Chelsea Flower Show and Chelsea in Bloom

> rhs.org.uk; chelseainbloom.co.uk

Nothing quite prepares you for the scale of the annual **Chelsea Flower Show**, a must on the horticultural enthusiast's calendar; its riotous colour, happy crowds – including many famous faces – and the sight of so much creative horticultural endeavour are as heady a mix as the scents of the multitudinous plants on show. It's come a long, long way since its first incarnation in 1913, when, as the Great Spring Show, it comprised a three-day event held within a single marquee. These days the 15 or so always original and often controversial Show and Sanctuary Gardens are surrounded by hundreds of exhibitors selling plants and all manner of horticulturally focused things you'd never

have imagined you might need, but covet as soon as you see them. The combination of inventive take-home ideas and planting as well as wildly imaginative designs makes Chelsea thrilling – and the star-spotting's a lot of fun, too. There's even late-night music and dancing with DJ Jo Whiley, an RHS Ambassador. Coinciding with the show is the week-long **Chelsea in Bloom** festival, which fills the wider area with floral-themed art in a competition that sees local businesses vie for the many coveted awards, among them best floral display and people's champion.

> *Tickets on sale in September*

Bike with the best
Ford RideLondon

> ridelondon.co.uk

Held over the last Bank Holiday weekend of May, the **Ford RideLondon-Essex 100** is cycling's equivalent of the London Marathon, and it's a daunting challenge – 100 miles of road riding through the capital and the villages of Essex before a hopefully triumphant return to central London, which most of the 20,000 riders achieve in an impressive five to seven hours. Mindful of the fact that very few of the capital's amateur cyclists will be up for such a gruelling event, RideLondon also offers a handful of gentler rides in the 60-mile and 30-mile routes, which incorporate some of the 100's route, along with the family-friendly Freecycle event, held entirely in the centre of the city. All events give cyclists the chance to experience the fun and freedom of cycling on traffic-free roads in London, with the Freecycle event adding a party atmosphere in its two festival zones (at Bank and St Paul's).

> *Tickets on sale in November/December for the 100 and on sale in October for the 60 and 30*

Enjoy thrill-a-minute cricket
T20 (Twenty20)

> tickets.surreycricket.com

Cricket purists may pooh-pooh it, but **T20**, a shortened format game, held between May and September, makes one of sport's most impenetrable games accessible to everyone, even if you can't tell your googly from your Google. Put simply, the traditional four- or five-day match is truncated to just 20 overs, or 120 legal balls, in a matter of two to three hours. From these overs, the batting team must score as many points as they can, with the emphasis on runs rather than wickets, meaning they go 'hell for leather'. Surrey and Middlesex teams play their home matches during the tournament at the capital's The Oval and Lord's, respectively. To be part of the 30,000-strong crowd at the latter is one of the best experiences you can have as a sports' fan, whether you're at the Pavilion End or the Nursery End. A Super Early Bird window is open from January until February, with tickets usually available until late spring from the grounds' websites. And if you're not sure what to plump for, the Friday night matches are a riot.

> Tickets on sale in January

Experience the best of Britain's emerging creative talent at art college shows
Degree Shows

> creativereview.co.uk

London's art colleges have produced some of the world's greatest modern artists. In fine art, the likes of Peter Blake, Barbara Hepworth, David Hockney, Tracey Emin and Damian Hirst have all come through world-famous schools such as the Royal College of Art and Chelsea School of Art. In fashion, Stella McCartney, John Galliano and the late Alexander McQueen all studied at, where else, Central St Martins. And in filmmaking, music and other creative forms, practitioners such as Jarvis Cocker, Joe Wright, P J Harvey and Ridley Scott all discovered their talents across the capital, at schools such as Camberwell, Wimbledon, Goldsmiths, Chelsea and Slade. The **degree shows** at these establishments are a great way to experience first-hand the early work of future creative titans, and they're free. Shows usually start in May and continue through June. The best place to find specific dates and details is via the Creative Review website, which publishes a guide each spring.

Explore the magic of string theory
Covent Garden May Fair and Puppet Festival

> facebook.com/MayFayreOnline

Put aside notions of wife-beating Mr Punch (these days the focus is more on slapstick humour, and modern Punch and Judy 'Professors' have toned down and developed the material to take in modern sensibilities) for this jubilant free celebration of the art of puppetry. Held in the Garden of St Paul's Church, near the spot where diarist Samuel Pepys first recorded sighting the forebear of Mr Punch in 'an Italian puppet play' on

9 May 1662, it brings together puppeteers from around the world to show their skills. The anarchic Punch is still a major part of the proceedings, taking part in a church service at noon after a grand procession around the neighbourhood led by the Superior Brass Band. Workshops, stalls, live music and maypole dancing lend the whole afternoon the kind of olde English folk experience generally only found in areas outside of the capital.

Snap up new photographic talent
Photo London

> photolondon.org

If you would like to catch the best of contemporary and historical international photography in one curated space, **Photo London**, held in a tent on the grounds of Somerset House, is the place to head. It's generally held over a long weekend in mid-May, and the main space is filled with exhibitors largely hailing from London, but also, in past shows, from Lima, Buenos Aires, Hong Kong, Warsaw, New York, Helsinki, Toronto, Istanbul, Shanghai, Sydney, Tehran and Ljubljana. There are satellite exhibitions dedicated to individual photographers and themes too: in 2024, French photographer Valérie Belin and a celebration of early French photography were two strong examples. A feature of the show are several awards, including the Master of Photography Award, honouring a living artist who'd made an outstanding contribution to the form. Of note is also the Photo London x Nikon Emerging Photographer Award, which highlights works of outstanding young practitioners at the fair and presents a special display dedicated to the previous year's winner.

Catch a match
Live Football

> thefa.com

Let's face it, a dream ticket to either the women's or the men's FA Cup Finals at Wembley Stadium is beyond the reach of all but the most loyal supporters or the super-rich prepared to shell out eye-watering amounts for a hospitality package. But if you're happy to consider a different event or venue, there are ways of seeing **live football** at all price points. If it has to be Wembley, then international matches featuring England, particularly friendlies, tend to have better availability, as do matches featuring the Lionesses. If you're less fussed about the hallowed turf, London's Premier League teams run membership schemes which can occasionally get you a ticket to a less popular game. Outside of that top division you can book tickets for clubs such as Queen's Park Rangers or Leyton Orient with relative ease. The lower down the leagues you go, the more availability there is – and the more the price goes down. For example, Haringey Borough, who play their home matches in Tottenham, run a free season ticket scheme which has boosted their match attendance and support in their neighbourhood.

Ready, set, go . . . to the city's most vibrant half-marathon
Wizz Air Hackney Half

> hackneymoves.com

The east London Borough of Hackney is one of the city's most diverse – and also one of its most densely populated with runners. It's a winning combination that makes this annual half-marathon one of the most exuberant and lively events in the capital's running calendar, with locals coming out in their thousands to cheer on friends, family, neighbours and visitors alike. If you're hoping to participate, it's worth noting that the 24,000 spaces for the half-marathon go fast once registration opens in March, but if you miss out there's still the chance to run for a charity – details of which are all on the website. Adults and kids aged 13 and over can take part in the Hackney 5k, and children aged 4 to 11 can run in the Schools' Challenge (both held on a Saturday). There's lots of entertainment along the route, but for a festival vibe, the Event Village, housed on Hackney Marshes (which is the start point for the races), offers live music, street food and activities for all.

> *Registration information available in May*

Shakespeare and so much more outdoors
Regent's Park Open Air Theatre

> openairtheatre.com

The oldest professional, permanent outdoor theatre in Britain used to be a paean to the comedic work of Shakespeare played out in the balmy, bucolic environs of Regent's Park, with the likes of *A Midsummer Night's Dream, Twelfth Night, The Taming of the Shrew* and *Love's Labour's Lost* firm favourites on a programme that began its first full season in 1933 – and continued during the war. These days, the annual 18-week season offers a much broader range of productions, from Stephen Sondheim musicals and classics such as *Gigi* and

High Society to Gilbert & Sullivan operas. Straight theatre is popular too, with top-tier performances by stars in productions such as *The Importance of Being Earnest, The Crucible* and *To Kill a Mockingbird* adding their appeal and drawing crowds of 140,000 each year. Which to choose? Hearing birdsong in the trees around you as twilight falls is a magical experience, and never more so than when watching one of Shakespeare's comedies.

Serpentine Gallery Pavilion (designed
by Jean Nouvel, 2010), page 89

June

Get the keys to London's most coveted secret spaces
London Open Gardens

> londongardenstrust.org

If you've ever passed one of those alluring gated gardens or squares that London's full of and glimpsed inside, wishing you could cross its locked portals, the weekend-long **London Open Gardens** is a must, offering public access to more than a hundred secret or usually closed green spaces. And it's not just gated gardens that are made accessible; over the 30 years the event has been running, spaces have expanded from the visible to the totally hidden – taking in exquisite roof gardens owned by City banks and private institutions and even the Prime Minister's Downing Street garden. Myriad styles cover everything from country cottage and expansive borders to new and experimental landscape design. So popular are some of the gardens that entry to them is only by individual ballot, but a weekend ticket gives access to all the remaining gardens over both days. Early bird tickets are available from January.

> *Tickets on sale in January*

Take Pride in London
Pride in London Parade

> prideinlondon.org

London's LGBTQIA+ community marches loud and proud on its colourful **Pride in London Parade** through the capital's centre on the last Saturday of June, with lots of free activities and performances in and around Trafalgar Square. And the activities aren't restricted to just one day; the month-long Pride Festival leading up to the big day takes in cabaret, theatre, film, talks, exhibitions, live music and more. Advance registration to take part in the parade begins in early December of the preceding year, ending in late January, and it's popular – in 2023, an estimated 35,000 participants whooped it up on central London's streets. If you miss the cut-off date, you could consider volunteering to help run the event; more than 1,000 volunteers are needed on the day to ensure a great festival, and the bright 'Pride in London' steward T-shirt is definitely a keeper.

> *Parade registration opens in December*

Anyone for tennis?
Cinch Championships

> lta.org.uk

Enjoy some hot musical collaborations
Meltdown Festival

> southbankcentre.co.uk

These days the **Cinch Championships**, formerly known as Queen's, after the venue it's held at each year, is almost as hard to get tickets to as Wimbledon, but it's that 'almost' that makes the difference between seeing world famous tennis players such as high-ranking Carlos Alcaraz in action on TV or live on one of the two show courts that make up this West Kensington venue. Established in 1889 and usually held in the latter half of June, the tournament is consistently attended by the best singles and doubles players of the men's game, and if you sign up for a £20 Advantage Fan+ account, you'll gain entry to priority booking windows for this event and all Lawn Tennis Association championships – including Wimbledon. Ground, unreserved Court 1 tickets and evening tickets are very reasonably priced, while centre court tickets start from around £50 (at time of writing).

> *Priority tickets on sale in February*

The idea of getting a composer or musician to curate a personal music festival across London's iconic South Bank Centre spaces first emerged more than 30 years ago, with modern classical composers George Benjamin, Louis Andriessen and Magnus Lindberg sealing their place in **Meltdown**'s pantheon of greats as its first curators. In the mid-nineties the festival's focus expanded beyond classical. Since then the likes of Elvis Costello, Yoko Ono (pictured), Nick Cave, David Byrne, Grace Jones and Chaka Khan have put together an eclectic and unique programme of acts and collaborations – perhaps most notably in 2007, when an all-star line-up including Nick Cave, Grace Jones and Pete Doherty took to the stage with curator Jarvis Cocker to perform a set comprised of Disney songs! The festival usually takes place over two weeks in mid- to late-June, with line-up announcements beginning in spring, and tickets on sale shortly after. Sign up to the South Bank Centre newsletter to be the first to hear about both.

Catch the largest open submission exhibition in the world
Royal Academy Summer Exhibition

> royalacademy.org.uk

Held every year since 1769, the **Royal Academy Summer Exhibition**, running from June to August, showcases an eye-popping, broad range of contemporary artworks, all chosen by a coordinator (in 2024 sculptor Ann Christopher RA, in 2018 Grayson Perry), aided by a panel of Academicians. The works that make it through their fascinating selection process (try to catch Joe Lycett's lively documentary *Summer Exhibitionist* before visiting to see how it's all done) to cover the walls and floors of the Piccadilly space span prints, paintings, films, photography, sculpture and architectural works, and there truly is something for everyone among the mix of art by household names and emerging talent. It's this mix that makes the exhibition such fun, and the fact that much of the work is for sale, with prices ranging from less than £100 to utterly silly money, just adds to the experience.

> *Submissions open in January*

Forget Edinburgh and enjoy London's very own arts festival

Summer by the River Festival

> londonbridgecity.co.uk

Having morphed from the smaller month-long free The Scoop festival, held since 2003 at a purpose-built 1,000-seater amphitheatre on the banks of the Thames, the three-month-long **Summer by the River Festival** has also expanded on the original's ever-eclectic and bold mix of highbrow to eyebrow-raising theatre and live arts. This festival offers a huge array of free events across three riverside locations – The Scoop, Hay's Galleria and The Pier. Between them, there really is something for everyone, from Tuesday night film screenings and Thursday new music nights to live theatre, pop-up

events and big-screen action showings of the summer's big sporting events, including of course, tennis lovers' Wimbledon. Bars, food stands and a wonderfully laidback feel to the al fresco events guarantee a good evening – though this being London, you may want to bring a blanket … hopefully to sit on rather than to wrap yourself in.

Immerse yourself in the best of global design
London Design Biennale

> londondesignbiennale.com

Held over three weeks every other June in the lovely courtyard and galleries of Somerset House, the **London Design Biennale** is a fascinating showcase for the role of global design in creating universal solutions to problems that concern us all. Since its inception, hundreds of designers from around the world have delivered multifaceted and inventive responses to themes overseen by an iconic artistic director – in 2021, the multi-award-winning artist and designer Es Devlin, who chose the theme 'Resonance', in 2023, the Dutch Nieuwe Instituut, which chose the theme of 'The Global Game:

Remapping Collaborations'. Sounds dry as a bone? It really isn't: many of the installations and exhibitions sit at the intersection of art and design to deliver beautiful pieces that are as mesmerising as they are original. Automorph Network's *Creative Differences*, Turkey's *Open Work* and the *Inner Peace Pavilion* from 2023 are great examples. Biennale Forum and Biennale Sessions, a dynamic programme of talks, workshops, screenings, roundtables and performances, offer added context and insights.

Get down to the beat in Brockwell
Brockwell Live

> brockwell-live.com;

The umbrella organisation **Brockwell Live** puts on five music festivals each year in the run-up to South London's Lambeth Country Show (see page 86). It all begins in mid-May with the best of UK electronica, rap, hip-hop and bass music at Project 6 from the team behind Outlook Festival and Undivide, followed by Wide Awake, covering all things indie, including post-punk, electronica and techno – and, in 2022, voted the NME's Best Small Festival of the Year. Over the Bank Holiday weekend Cross the Tracks offers soul, jazz and funk and City Splash reggae, Afrobeats and dancehall, with the pop and LGBTQIA+ sensibilities of Mighty Hoopla, once awarded Time Out's Best London festival, bringing festivities to a close over the first weekend of June. It's all incredibly well organised and has a nice community-focused feel, with a free family festival, discounted group tickets and locals tickets that give early access to the site, and line-ups are always an engaging mix of classy headliners and the best up-and-coming talent around.

> *Brockwell Park, Brixton;*
> *mid-May to early June*

Sample the best of London's cuisine
Taste of London

> london.tastefestivals.com

The capital's multicultural mix makes it a paradise for global food, and nowhere can the breadth of it be sampled more easily than at the annual **Taste of London** food festival. Held in Regent's Park over five days, it brings together restaurants, chefs, producers and foodies for a feast of activities as disparate as craft beer and cider trails, cookery classes with Michelin-starred chefs, cocktail masterclasses, firepit singalong sessions and live DJ sets. There's plenty to sample across the site and even more to buy at the different markets. A wide range of ticket options span basic entry and tasting tickets (including two dishes), through to multiple entry passes and, top of the pile, a VIP three-dish package with includes access to exclusive events and areas, plus fast-track entry.

> *Hyde Park; mid-June*

Sample a slice of medieval history
Barnet Medieval Festival

> barnetmedievalfestival.org

The outer northern London borough of Barnet may not look like it holds an important part in English history, but looks can be deceiving. For it was here, more than 550 years ago, that the Battle of Barnet took place (on 14 April 1471), a decisive encounter in the Wars of the Roses in which the Yorkist army of Edward IV defeated the Lancastrian forces led by Warwick 'the Kingmaker'. The battle is reenacted by up to 300 participants, who not only engage in hand-to-hand combat, archery, cannon firing and other battle acts but also take part in more day-to-day activities to offer insights into how life was lived in the fifteenth century. Stalls like the Olde Roving Apothecary, selling things like medieval pickles, add to the fun, and kids get the chance to dress up, wield wooden swords and learn how to paint shields.

Revel in some special musical moments
Spitalfields Festival

> spitalfieldsmusic.org.uk

Run by Spitalfields Music, a charity that aims to bring east London communities together through music, the **Spitalfields Festival** takes place over two weeks in late June/early July. The remit is classical music from the last 500 years plus specially commissioned new works. The standard of musicianship is high, and events take place in atmospheric, historic venues. Thoughtfully curated concerts have featured protest songs through the ages, from Franz Schubert to Benjamin Britten, staged at Shoreditch Church. Another concert, held at the Tower of London's Church of St Peter ad Vincula, took inspiration from the Tudors, with pieces from contemporary American composer Libby Larsen, as well as a sixteenth-century choral work by Thomas Tallis. Walks and talks are also part of the line-up. Events usually sell out, especially the ones in the Tower of London, so move fast when tickets go on sale in April.

> *Tickets on sale in April*

Build a different view of how cities work
London Festival of Architecture

> londonfestivalofarchitecture.org

The fact that this month-long celebration of architecture and city-making has been going strong for more than 20 years is a testament to its ability to connect a sometimes seemingly inaccessible profession with an audience who clearly feel engaged with its absorbing programme. Each year focuses on a particular theme, around which an imaginative range of 400 events, including talks, tours, installations and performances are gathered together. In 2014 for example, it was London's historic and modern architectural landmarks, with visitors taken on walks round the Gherkin and Centrepoint, jogging tours of the Olympic Fringes and sunset boat trips down the Thames, while an impressive line-up of speakers included Will Self, Yinka Shonibare and Lisa Jardine. Other years have seen equally compelling themes, such as 2006's notion of change, the most enduring memory of which was surely Richard Rogers and Renzo Piano driving 60 sheep across the Millennium Bridge, surrounded by more than 15,000 Londoners.

Catch a film in the capital under the stars
Summer Film Screenings

> thelunacinema.com
> rooftopfilmclub.com

Despite the variable weather, there are a surprising number of outdoor cinema options in London. Most prolific is Luna Cinema, which has outdoor screens all over London, at such great venues as Kew Gardens, Hampton Court, Clapham Common and Regent's Park Open Air Theatre. From June to September, they show crowd-pleasers and family favourites such as *Top Gun: Maverick* and *Paddington*. The most central setting is probably the Barbican's Sculpture Court, where over a couple of weeks, in late August, a great mix of films (anything from Tarkovsky's *Mirror* to *Singin' in the Rain*) is screened in their Outdoor Cinema series. On Tuesday evenings, from June to August, Canada Square Park, in east London, hosts screenings of popular films. On the same night in June and July, The Scoop at More London sunken outdoor amphitheatre, near Tower Bridge, shows a similar line-up of box office hits as part of the London Bridge City Summer by the River festival. Finally, the Rooftop Film Club starts showing films in late April, from venues in Peckham and Stratford.

> *For Summer by the River, see page 78.*

Get a slug of American baseball
MLB World Tour

> mlb.com

Major League Baseball (MLB) World Tour doesn't come to London every June, but when it does, the London Series sets up camp in the London Stadium for two games, and brings with it all the razzmatazz associated with the American sport. There are giant mascots, musical entertainment and a host of food outlets selling a range of American ballpark-style foodstuffs – from nachos and pizzas to giant hot dogs. Games usually last about 2.5 hours but run longer if a winner hasn't emerged after nine innings. In 2024, the packed east London stadium saw the New York Mets and Philadelphia Phillies go head-to-head. MLB only began playing outside of America in 1996, when teams went to Mexico for three games. It came to London for the first time in 2019, when arch-rivals the Yankees and the Red Sox competed. Note that tickets go on sale in November for pre-registered fans, and December to the general public.

> *Tickets on sale in November (pre-registered fans) and December (general public)*

Enjoy a larger-than-life village fair
Lambeth Country Show

> lambethcountryshow.co.uk

For a weekend in early June, Brockwell Park is turned into an unlikely but rather wonderful country showground. It's a brilliant community event, attracting 120,000 people and more than 200 stalls – and it's free. There really is something for everyone: birds of prey displays, motorcycle stunts, jousting, tea dances, craft and music workshops, and all kinds of street food options. Musical entertainment runs from steel and samba bands and local choirs to international artists. Saturday sees funk soul and disco acts, while Sunday has ska, dub and reggae, and there's a dedicated Latino stage too. Rural life is represented by the sheep-centred Best in Show (Saturday only), which features a whole roster of classes, 25 different breeds and sheep-shearing demonstrations. There are also tents hosting more than 80 vegetable and flower competitions, including the much-loved and endlessly inventive Vegetable Sculpture category. There's also an Eco Village, where visitors can learn how to live more sustainably from organisations such as the London Beekeepers' Organisation and the London Wildlife Trust.

Admire the pageantry and the marching bands
Trooping the Colour

> kbp.army.mod.uk

JUN

This military ceremony marks the official birthday of the sovereign. Proceedings start at 10 a.m. on a Saturday in mid-June, when the monarch rides from Buckingham Palace to Horse Guards Parade to inspect the troops, before over 1,400 soldiers and 200 horses put on an impressive display to the sound of ten military bands. The King then returns to the palace to watch an RAF flypast at 1 p.m. There's also a 41-gun salute fired from Green Park. Apply for tickets (awarded by ballot, no more than four per applicant) from March, and note that there's a dress code. Those without a ticket can enjoy the loud, live music and see the troops (all in full ceremonial uniform) marching along the Mall - a sight to behold - or try for a view of the parade ground from the edge of St James's Park. There are also two other **Trooping the Colour** ceremonies on Saturdays in June at which the monarch isn't present. Tickets for these ceremonies are cheaper and easier to obtain.

> *Tickets from March (by ballot)*

Experience live storytelling
Barnes Children's Literature Festival

> barneskidslitfest.org

Go the distance (or simply spectate) for charity
London to Brighton Cycle Ride

> bhf.org.uk
> londonbrightoncycle.co.uk

The biggest children's book festival in the UK takes place in Barnes, in south-west London, every summer, over a weekend in late June. It packs a lot into that time – many of the big names in children's literature appearing, including Michael Rosen, poet, author and broadcaster, known for *We're Going on a Bear Hunt*, Axel Scheffler and Julia Donaldson, respectively the illustrator and author of iconic *The Gruffalo*, Lauren Child, creator of *Charlie and Lola*, Michael Morpurgo, most famous for *War Horse*, and Cressida Cowell, author of *How to Train Your Dragon*. As well as talks, discussions, storytelling and signings, there are interactive events and performances, such as *Borka*, a family-friendly opera, *Roald Dahl & the Imagination Seekers*, a show involving games and immersive storytelling, and Baby Broadway, a dance- and sing-along to songs from musicals for ages 0-8 and their parents. The festival takes place in various venues in Barnes, including the Judith Kerr Marquee pitched on Barnes Green. A weekend of immense fun and imagination.

The iconic 55-mile bike ride from Clapham Common to Brighton seafront, in Sussex, is used by more than one organisation as a fundraiser. The British Heart Foundation has been running one in June for more than 45 years, the one held in September is in aid of a collection of charities, and has been going for 15 years or so. For both, the entry fee buys the ride, plus a souvenir medal at the finish line. Participants must be 16 or over. Early bird tickets cost £55 in 2024; riding for a specific charity means the entry fee is cheaper but you have to commit to raising a certain amount of money for them. There's lots of support both before and during the race, from tips on how to prepare, to rest stops along the way offering water refills and toilets and staffed with mechanics (though riders are expected to be able to mend their own punctures). Riders set off in staggered stages from 6 in the morning and the toughest section comes near the end, when riders face the climb to Ditchling Beacon.

> *Tickets on sale in March*

Appreciate stellar architecture
Serpentine Pavilion

> serpentinegalleries.org

Every year since 2000, an international architect has been commissioned to design a temporary pavilion next to Serpentine South in Kensington Gardens. Over the years, some of the world's most renowned architects have taken part – the only proviso is that it has to be their first built structure in England. Zaha Hadid designed the first pavilion and went on to transform an old military building into what's now Serpentine North in 2013. Three years earlier, architect Jean Nouvel dreamed up a geometric vision in post box red; artist Olafur Eliasson and architect Kjetil Thorsen collaborated on a timber-clad structure that looked like an glossy pixie hat in 2007; in 2015, it was a colourful plastic pavilion designed by SelgasCano; and Oscar Niemeyer's earlier 2003 design was an elegant steel, aluminium, concrete and glass construction, with a partly submerged auditorium. The temporary pavilions stay from early June to mid October and are always worth spending time in. Whatever the design, there's seating and a refreshment hub, and delightful architectural details and exhibitions to contemplate in lovely environs.

London music festivals: a round-up

London's music festivals are some of the best in Europe. Usually held in the city's parks, they're intimate, friendly and, often, free, while those that do charge usually offer discounted tickets for locals and/or community events around the actual festival. Tickets generally go on sale a few months before the big day, and signing up to a festival's mailing list ensures early notification of when that is and how to get tickets. Here are some popular favourites.

Barnes Music Festival

> Various venues, Barnes;
  barnesmusicfestival.com; March

Across a fortnight in March, international stars and local groups and schools perform an accessible and varied mix of choral, instrumental, orchestral, opera, jazz and film music at venues across the south-west London area.

Pitchfork Music Festival

> Various venues, London; pitchforkmusicfestival.
  co.uk; November

This relative newcomer to the capital's music festival scene brings a welcome burst of new music at affordable prices in a range of venues across the capital, from small churches in Hackney to well-known venues like the Royal Albert Hall and purpose-built spaces such as Kings Place, where in 2023 US National Youth Poet Laureate and singer/songwriter Kara Jackson was just one of the acts performing a mesmerising set.

Ealing Summer Festivals

> Walpole Park; ealingsummerfestivals.com;
  mid-July to early August

The London Borough of Ealing offers locals and visitors not one, not two, but three weekend festivals in Walpole Park each year, kicking off in mid-July with a Comedy Festival and continuing into late July with the Blues festival, before closing in the first weekend of August with the Jazz Festival.

La Linea – The London Latin Music Festival

> Various venues; comono.co.uk; April

Since its launch in 2001, La Linea has been bringing a broad range of Latin performers to a range of large and small venues across the capital - including the Barbican, St James's Church, Rio Cinema and the Jazz Café.

We are FSTVL

> Dagenham; wearefstvl.com; last weekend of May

Now in its second decade, this electronic dance music festival is becoming more and more popular - helped by the good tube links which make it accessible to audiences. In 2024 the line-up featured some of the biggest names in the genre, with the likes of Eric Prydz, Chase and Status and Jamie Jones giving the crowd a Bank Holiday weekend to remember.

West End LIVE

> Trafalgar Square, westendlive.co.uk; late June

Westminster City Council and the Society of London Theatre come together each year to put on this weekend of live music from London's West End musicals, and it's all free and unticketed. Must-sees as well as new shows are covered among some fifty performances over the two days.

Brick Lane Jazz Festival

> Truman Brewery and nearby venues; bricklanejazzfestival.com; Late April

This three-day weekend of jazz across ten East End venues (most of them less than a couple of minutes' walk from the central Truman Brewery hub) offers a festival pass giving admittance to all its 100+ gigs, along with a day pass. Both operate on a first-come, first-served basis.

South Facing

> Crystal Palace Park; southfacingfestival.com; July and August

Head to Crystal Palace for two weeks of eclectic outdoor concerts at the Park's Bowl amphitheatre. In 2024, Grace Jones headlined the new disco, soul and electronic all-dayer Love Motion, with other acts across the fortnight including Dancehall sensation Popcaan, who brings Unruly Fest, his day-long celebration of Jamaican music and culture, to the party. Past headliners have included Jungle and Richard Ashcroft.

Somerset House Summer Series

> Somerset House; somersethouse.org.uk; July

A firm favourite on the London indie music scene for its intimate courtyard setting, this 11-night series of concerts always delivers, with past headliners including Amy Winehouse, Adele, Underworld, The XX, Florence and The Machine, Soul2Soul, Alison Goldfrapp, Young Fathers, Arlo Parks, The Prodigy and Patti Smith.

GALA Festival

> Peckham Rye Park; thisisgala.co.uk; last weekend of May

Held over the three days of the late-May Bank Holiday weekend, this long-running dance music festival encompasses house, techno, jungle, drum 'n' bass, jazz, disco and more, with lots of community-focused events thrown into the mix.

Wembley Park Live

> Various venues, Wembley; wembleypark.com; April-September

This free festival of live music at a range of venues - including Wembley BoxPark and The Sound Shell at Wembley Park - is a community-focused affair that showcases young talent and more.

Hampton Court Palace Festival

> Hampton Court;
hamptoncourtpalacefestival.com; June

The series of summer concerts held in this royal palace are totally top-notch; the 2024 line-up featured no less than Sir Tom Jones and Nile Rodgers & Chic, while past acts over its 28-year history have included such luminaries as Kylie, The Beach Boys, Liza Minnelli, Elton John, Gladys Knight and Grace Jones.

Wireless Festival

> Finsbury Park; wirelessfestival.co.uk; mid-July

Hear the best of rap, R&B, grime, hip-hop and more at this celebration of urban music. Past line-ups have featured some of its biggest names – in 2024 Nicki Minaj, 21 Savage and Doja Cat, with other years offering Travis Scott, Playboi Carti and D-Block Europe.

Kaleidoscope

> Alexandra Palace Park; kaleidoscope-festival.com; mid-July

The acts on stages across the sweeping ground of Ally Pally create a programme packed with live music and DJ sets at this one-day event, which also features a comedy tent and a dedicated family area filled with arts and crafts, theatre and circus activities.

All Points East

> Victoria Park, Hackney;
allpointseastfestival.com; August

Two weekends of music across two stages bookend In the Neighbourhood, a four-day-long free community event of performance, activities, food and outdoor film screenings. This longstanding festival, in the past, has included everyone from Kraftwerk, Björk, Foals and The Chemical Brothers to, most recently, Ezra Collective, Loyle Carner and Kaytranada.

Summer opening of Buckingham
Palace, page 102

July

Get inspired at this relaxed horticultural bonanza
Hampton Court Palace Garden Festival

> rhs.org.uk

Run by the Royal Horticultural Society, this celebration of gardens runs for six days in early July in the grounds of Hampton Court Palace. The show has a more relaxed vibe than the Chelsea Flower Show (and tickets are certainly easier to come by). Children are welcome and there are family trails and activities such as den building to keep them entertained. Non-gardening attractions include musicians on the bandstand, street food stalls and plenty of Champagne and Pimm's. Beautiful show gardens range from exquisite formal designs to equally appealing ones filled with budget ideas or plants ready to meet the challenges of climate change. The RHS Allotment garden is a popular attraction, too. The huge Floral Marquee (6,750 sq. m) is filled with plants and flowers from over 90 nurseries. The Plant Village offers an opportunity to buy. There are workshops and talks to help budding gardeners progress, and inspiration in the form of Get Started Gardens.

> *Tickets on sale in March*

Picnic to the sounds of pop
Kew the Music

> kewthemusic.org

A series of picnic-concerts, taking place over a week in July, in the bucolic surroundings of Kew Gardens. Visitors can bring their own picnics, or take advantage of the on-site bars and food stalls; blankets and folding chairs are allowed (though the organisers draw the line at tables, tents and gazebos). There are different musicians (with support acts) on each night, and 2024 saw performances from former boy-band JLS, pop star Mika, singer-songwriters Beverley Knight and Ronan Keating, and Richard Ashcroft, best known as lead singer of The Verve. Weather permitting, it's a very civilised way of listening to well-known acts in an almost-festival setting.

> *Tickets on sale in February*

Inspect some splendid vintage vehicles
Cart-marking

> thecarmen.co.uk

This celebration of an ancient tradition is one of the best of the quaint ceremonies that take place in the City of London over the year. The annual **cart-marking** ceremony is on a Saturday in July and is organised by the Worshipful Company of Carmen and attended by dignitaries such as the Lord Mayor. Marking is an old form of licensing – once, the carts themselves would be branded: these days the red-hot iron brands a piece of wood temporarily attached to the vehicles. Spectators get to admire 40 or so handsome vehicles at close range. Vintage lorries, veteran motorcycles, horse-drawn carts, retro delivery vans and a few modern vehicles queue to get into the Guildhall Yard, where the ceremony takes place. It usually starts at 10 a.m. and lasts for a couple of hours. The vehicles patiently wait their turn in the streets around Guildhall – position yourself on Gresham Street for a prime view.

Relish pomp and ceremony for an ancient military tradition
Beating Retreat

> tickets.householddivision.org.uk

Explore the most unusual artists' studios in London
Eel Pie Island Open Studios

> eelpieislandartists.co.uk
> eelpiemuseum.co.uk

Beating Retreat is a ceremony that has its origins in the command for troops to retreat, or return. It is now a magnificent pageant involving military bands, precision marching, cannons and fireworks. The Household Division consists of the seven British Army Regiments serving the King, and their Beating Retreat runs over three evenings in July, on Horse Guards Parade, and is billed as 'A Military Musical Spectacular'. In 2024, the Bands of the Household Division, Massed Pipes and Drums and the Mounted State Trumpeters of the Household Cavalry all took part. The 80th anniversary of the D-Day landings was commemorated, while the music paid homage to rock artists of Great Britain.

> *Tickets on sale in February*

Held on two weekends a year (the second in December), this **Open Studios** event is a great way of seeing and buying original artists' work, as well as a fine opportunity to explore Eel Pie Island. Accessed by a footbridge from Twickenham, and cut off during very high tides, Eel Pie Island is a quirky remnant from a more bohemian age. Twenty or so artists and craftspeople live or work there, including fine artists, ceramicists, illustrators, mosaicists and jewellers. Check out the Eel Pie Island Museum in Twickenham before your visit for some background on this intriguing place.

Watch tennis stars at the top of their game
Wimbledon Championships

> wimbledon.com

The oldest tennis tournament in the world is as much a social occasion as it is a sporting fixture, but there's no doubt that the tennis there is world class. Centre Court tickets for the finals of the Singles Championships are the dream, but some of the most entertaining tennis can be found elsewhere: the boys or girls matches (where you can see the stars of the future) or the Invitation Doubles (where there's a chance to watch a retired favourite player). On the outer courts, spectators are very close to the action, while on the show courts the seats are slightly further away from the courts, but the atmosphere everywhere is electric. In between the games, there are plenty of opportunities for Pimm's, Champagne, strawberries and souvenirs. There's also a museum on site. Tickets are by ballot, but a limited number (one per person) are sold each day. Join the queue by 9 a.m. and you're in with a chance. Or arrive later and queue for vacated seats. Or you could watch the Championships on one of the many big screens dotted around London.

> *Tickets are available by ballot from late September to mid-October of the previous year; limited numbers are sold on the day.*

Catch legendary acts in 'The People's Park'
BST Hyde Park

> bst-hydepark.com

Going strong for more than ten years, the American Express-sponsored **BST Hyde Park** shows no sign of running out of steam. Held in London's most central Park, the site of many important historic events, from the suffragettes' orations and the Great Exhibition to the first Pride march, audiences now pack together, across multiple weekends, to watch a mix of global musical legends perform. Bruce Springsteen, Elton John, Billy Joel, Andrea Bocelli, Pink, Take That, Kings of Leon and South Korean megastars Stray Kids are among those who've taken to the stage in the past. Amex card holders can register early for tickets, which span a wide range of packages at equally wide-ranging price points, but if you don't want to fork out the money to get into the site you can take a picnic and enjoy the sounds floating across the rest of Hyde Park, if the wind's right. And that's not all, the free midweek programme Open House includes an outdoor cinema, Wimbledon screenings, Virgin Active Workout sessions, nature and learning workshops, arts and crafts, a Street Food Market, pop-up bars and live music. There's pretty much something for everyone.

> *Amex presale tickets on sale in February*

Savour the pace at a long cricket match
Test Cricket in London

> lords.org
> kiaoval.com

London offers two great venues in which to see test match cricket: Lord's and the Oval. Lord's hosts two men's team matches a season (May to September) and the Oval, one. Unlike the thrill-a-minute shorter games, a test match lasts up to five days and you can buy tickets for the first four days in advance via the respective websites – members get priority but with planning it's possible to pick up tickets. Be warned, they're not cheap, but, certainly for the last day, they are possible to pick up. Due to the fact that test matches can finish before the fifth day, tickets for that day don't usually go on sale until the end of the fourth day, so even if you haven't bought tickets in advance for a sold out match you still have a chance of getting in. Both grounds host other matches throughout the summer in a variety of formats, including women's international cricket (although these are currently much less frequent).

> *Registration open from January*

Peek into the life of the Royals
Buckingham Palace State Rooms' Opening

> rct.uk

Each summer, from July to September, when the Royals head out of town to one of their many other properties around Britain, the State Rooms of their London residence are opened to all – at a price, of course. The 19 rooms, largely styled by George IV, who commissioned John Nash to design them in 1825, are the public rooms in which visiting dignitaries are received and entertained, and as you'd expect, are filled with the kinds of things we've all come to expect from watching *The Crown* – including paintings by Van Dyck and Canaletto, sculpture by Canova, Sèvres porcelain, and some of the finest English and French furniture in the world. The White Drawing Room is the grandest of the spaces, but don't miss the Throne Room and Music Room. Outside of the summer months, private guided tours take place regularly.

Be a 'prommer' at the world's most democratic musical festival
The Proms

> royalalberthall.com

Ever since its inauguration in 1895, when impresario Robert Newman realised his idea of democratising live concerts with low ticket prices and an informal atmosphere, the eight-week **Proms** festival of classical music and more has remained steadfastly affordable. This is particularly true if you're happy to 'promenade' in the standing areas of the Royal Albert Hall (the Arena and Gallery), where more than 1,000 single priced tickets (currently £8), are sold on a first-come, first-served basis for each concert, on the morning of the day it takes place. In more recent years the programme has become ever more eclectic and accessible, and while opinions are divided on this, the likes of Northern Soul and Sci-fi Film Music Proms alongside evergreen favourites like Holst's *The Planets*, Tchaikovsky's *Swan Lake* and Beethoven's *Fifth Symphony* combine to deliver a programme that continues to prove hugely popular. The big event, of course, is The Last Night of the Proms.

> *For The Last Night of the Proms, see page 114*

Music Festivals (Tame Impala at
All Points East, 2022), page 93

August

Enjoy spectacular outdoor performances for free
Greenwich+Docklands International Festival (GDIF)

> festival.org

It's hard to argue with the organisers' claim that the **Greenwich+Docklands International Festival** is 'London's leading festival of free outdoor theatre and performing arts'. Taking place over 17 days from late August to early September, you can expect amazing physical theatre, fireworks and spectacular lighting effects, community involvement and interactive performances. Recent hits have included Bandaloop's awe-inspiring vertical dance on the south façade of St Paul's Cathedral, Tatiana Mosio Bongonga's eye-popping tightrope walk over General Gordon Square in Woolwich and the sheer fun of Dancing City, a weekend's worth of dance performances, ranging from ballet to hip-hop, dotted around Canary Wharf. There are also plenty of community and family events. Greenwich Fair saw a host of circus, street arts, theatre, dance and circus acts take over the grounds of the Old Royal Naval College, Cutty Sark Gardens and Greenwich Park in an afternoon of fun. GDIF is part of the Royal Greenwich Festivals, a series of events celebrating cultural vibrancy and diversity.

Be bowled over watching action-packed cricket
The Hundred

> thehundred.com

Unmissable sporting events used to be thin on the ground in the dog days of summer, but then, in 2021, The Hundred was unleashed. Yes, it's cricket, but it's as far from the languid nature of a test match as it's possible to get. Instead, spectators get an action-packed, unmissable 100-ball cricket competition that, over five weeks of matches at grounds around the country, is whittled down to a final at Lord's that's as raucous as anything the Indian Premier League has to offer – except perhaps the passion of a Chennai Super Kings game. With a 25-ball powerplay given to each team at the beginning of their innings, things get off to a lively start from the off, and matches last a very engaging and accessible two to three hours rather than the five-day affairs of test matches. Extra keen fans can buy double header tickets covering back-to-back women's and men's matches. To be in with a shout for tickets, which span the gamut from seats in no-alcohol and family-friendly stands to corporate packages with all its bells and whistles, sign up on the website, download the app and keep your fingers crossed.

> See also Test Cricket in London, page 101; Voneus Village Cup, page 121

Watch the oldest boat race in the world
Doggett's Coat & Badge Wager

> doggettsrace.com

Thomas Doggett founded the **Doggett's Coat and Badge Wager** in 1715, in honour of the accession of King George I. Today what is the oldest boat race in the world is run by the Fishmongers' Company and the Company of Watermen and Lightermen of the River Thames. The route runs from London Bridge to Cadogan Pier in Chelsea (4.6 miles) and it takes between 25 and 30 minutes to complete. The fastest time so far recorded was in 1973 by Bobby Prentice: 23 minutes 22 seconds. Up to six apprentice watermen and lightermen – women included – compete in single sculls; if more than six enter, then heats are held before race day. They compete for the Doggett's scarlet coat and silver badge, hence the race's name, which the winner wears when they're presented at a grand banquet at Fishmongers' Hall in November. So, catch the race and watch a little piece of history in the making.

Take on a mini Triathlon
London T100

> t100triathlon.com

Formerly Challenge London Triathalon, which consisted of a gruelling 2k swim, 80k bike ride and 18k run, the **London T100**, held in late July, is now just one of eight triathlon races taking place across the globe, beginning in Miami in March and taking in Singapore, Las Vegas and Dubai, among others. Pros take on all eight races vying for the impressive prize pot of £5.5m and the crown of T100 World Champion, but anyone can have a go at the individual races, with London's one including a swim through Royal Victoria Dock and races around London's most memorable landmarks. Alongside the 100k race are a series of shorter options taking place over the weekend, ranging from the sprint (Swim 0.75k, bike 20k, run 5k) and Olympic (swim 1.5k, bike 40k, run 10k) to relays. All participants get a sustainable goodies bag and, hopefully, a hard-won and well-deserved sense of satisfaction.

Eat and make merry at Henry VIII's favourite palace

Hampton Court Palace Food Festival

> hrpfestivals.com

Held in the grounds of Hampton Court Palace, this festival is about more than just food and drink. There's plenty of that, of course, but there are also workshops, family activities (face-painting, horse and cart rides, vintage games) and a bandstand showcasing live music. For the ticket price, visitors get access to the historic palace and the 60 acres of well-tended gardens, too. Stalls sell everything from chilli sauces and cheese to fudge and honey. Street trucks mean you can graze on churros, grilled toasties or paella, or refuel with bubble tea or something stronger, such as artisanal cider or a cocktail. As the festival takes place at the end of August, there's plenty of ice-cream and cold beer available, not to mention deckchairs for you to take a rest after all that feasting. Henry VIII would be proud.

Catch a concert in the gardens of an Art Deco palace

Music on a Sunday at Eltham Palace

> english-heritage.org.uk

The wonderful 1930s Art Deco architecture of this former medieval royal palace makes it a must-visit in the summer, when the 19 acres of award-winning gardens are at their most glorious and the sunlight streams into the palace rooms to light up the gold décor and furnishings of spaces filled with curious and unusual features – among them a gold bathroom containing a gold mosaic niche in which sits a statue of the goddess Psyche. As the home of such notables as King Edward II in 1305 and, in the early 20th century, millionaires Stephen and Virginia Courtauld, it provides a fascinating mix of styles, history and modernity, not least in the early central heating of the purpose-built home of Mah-Jong, the couple's pet lemur. But on Sundays in July, there's an added appeal; live concerts are held in the gardens, with visitors invited to bring picnics and enjoy the music. There are plenty of activities through the summer for kids too.

Parade, party or handle pan at London's most famous festival

Notting Hill Carnival

> nhcarnival.org

The Notting Hill Carnival has come a long way since it began as a community-led children's festival in 1966, with the Bank Holiday weekend event now regularly attracting around a million visitors, making it second only to Brazil's Rio Carnival in size. For visitors and locals alike it's a must-see event on the London cultural calendar, with the iconic floats, parade costumes, drummers, live music, sound systems and associated events – notably the UK National Panorama Steelband Competition – offering a wonderfully eclectic and comprehensive view of Caribbean culture in the city. But even better than watching the festival live is taking part in it, and it's easier than you might think. Whether you want to parade the streets in feathers and sequins as part of a mas (masquerade) band or beat an adapted oil drum on a float, the Carnival website has details of how to participate in any number of activities.

London Design Festival (INTO
SIGHT installation, 2022), page 127

September

Immerse yourself in a national tradition
Last Night of the Proms

> royalalberthall.com

Something akin to a religious experience for many, the **Last Night of the Proms** marks the end of two months of music at the BBC Proms at the Royal Albert Hall. It's the climax of the concerts, including quintessentially British crowd-rousing favourites like *Pomp & Circumstance March No. 1* by Edward Elgar (which features 'Land of Hope and Glory'), 'Rule, Britannia!' and 'Jerusalem'. The concert is led by a star conductor, such as Marin Alsop, the first woman ever to conduct it. Many prommers sport fancy dress, and flag waving is allowed. The last night sells out every year. Still, there are ways to try for a much-prized ticket – see the website for details. If you fail, the BBC has full coverage on radio, TV and streaming services.

> *Pre-sales ticket ballot opens in June;*
> *remaining tickets available in mid-July.*

See accomplished works in an intriguing setting
Trinity Buoy Wharf Drawing Prize & Exhibition

> trinitybuoywharf.com

One of the most prestigious open exhibitions for drawing in the UK, the award now known as the **Trinity Buoy Wharf Drawing Prize** is announced at the end of September. A selection of the works is then on display for a couple of weeks at Trinity Buoy, an arts centre beside the Thames, before going on tour. Around 3,000 drawings are submitted annually, from which roughly 125 are exhibited. Alongside works on paper, there are drawings on textiles and other materials, plus moving images, by established artists as well as new practitioners, from all over the world. Entries can be submitted between March and June, and a shortlist is announced in late July. There are five awards: first and second prizes, a Student Award, a biennial Evelyn Williams Drawing Award and a Working Drawing Award, given to a piece of work involved in the process of architecture or design. The Prize has been the starting point for many a successful artist's career.

> *Submissions open in March*

Watch pucks fly around town
Ice Hockey Season

Ice hockey is fast and furious, and tickets are cheaper than for many sporting fixtures, making this a popular spectator sport. To see why fans are so keen, go and watch one of London's League teams in action. London clubs that play in the National Ice Hockey League (not all in the same division) are the Haringey Huskies (based at Alexandra Palace Ice Rink), the Streatham Ice Hockey Club (Streatham Ice Centre), the Lee Valley Lions (Lee Valley Ice Centre) and the Raiders and the Buccaneers (Sapphire Ice, in Romford). The season runs from September to March, and most games are on Saturday or Sunday nights. Both Streatham Ice Centre and the Lee Valley Ice Centre have been upgraded in recent years and boast Olympic-sized rinks. Tickets tend to sell out quickly so keep an eye out.

SEP

Experience a harvest festival with a difference

Pearly Kings and Queens Costermongers Harvest Festival

> pearlysociety.org.uk

The Pearly Kings and Queens of London hold an annual Harvest Festival – also known as Costermongers Harvest Festival – on the last Sunday in September. Participants assemble at 1.30 p.m. in Guildhall Yard in the City, where there's jollity in the form of marching bands, veteran cars, singalongs and morris dancing. Everyone is welcome, and it's a chance to see the elaborate costumes with hundreds of mother-of-pearl buttons up close. The Pearlies then proceed to St-Mary-le-Bow on Cheapside for the 3 p.m. Harvest Festival service; again, it's open to all.

Witness a small flock crossing Southwark Bridge
London Sheep Drive

> sheepdrive.london

One of the most entertaining of City 'traditions', the notion of a **Sheep Drive** as a yearly ritual, only came into being in 2013, organised by the Worshipful Company of Woolmen. It was a success, and the spectacle of a handful of sheep being driven over Southwark Bridge on a Sunday in late September has continued ever since. This charity event celebrates a Freeman of the City of London's right to bring sheep to market over the Thames toll free. Only Freemen of the City of London and their guests can actually participate in the drive, though there's always a celebrity present: Shaun the Sheep, Dames Barbara Windsor and Mary Berry have all made an appearance. A Livery Fair (held on Queen Street) accompanies the spectacle – enticements include sheep-shearing, rare breeds, stalls selling wool products, as well as food and drink, and demonstrations of traditional skills such as weaving.

Explore the city's unique and rarely accessible buildings
Open House London

> programme.openhouse.org.uk

For a few days in mid-September, buildings that are normally closed to the public are made accessible. Since the project started in 1992, **Open House** has grown to include more than 800 buildings, ranging from architect-designed private homes and tiny Calvinist chapels to big-hitters such as the BT Tower and the Foreign & Commonwealth Office. Some of the most interesting buildings aren't in the centre of town though – past festivals have revealed the architectural secrets of the Adobe Village playscape at Hounslow Heath Infant & Nursery School, the Baitul Futuh Mosque in Morden, Poplar's brutalist landmark Balfron Tower and the Southwark Integrated Waste Management Facility, one of Europe's most advanced recycling facilities, just off the Old Kent Road. There are associated free walks and talks too, such as Deptford's Black History before and after Windrush and Sugar and Spice and All Things Nice – a sensory-inspired walk around the Royal Albert Dock (including the Tate & Lyle Sugar Refinery). It's all free, but some sites require you to book.

Pick up a painting, or just people watch
Art Car Boot Fair (ACBF)

> artcarbootfair.com

As the name suggests, the **Art Car Boot Fair** is a cross between an art fair and a car boot sale. It's intended to be a day when artists and potential buyers can interact one-to-one. It's fun *and* there are bargains to be had. The Fair started in 2004 in Brick Lane, and now takes place at Lewis Cubitt Square, King's Cross, on a Saturday in early–mid September. Artists include established names (Jeremy Deller say, or Rankin) and up-and-comers, and work runs the gamut from fine art to street. All works are specifically commissioned for the event. As well as over 100 artists, there are performers, karaoke, a bar, plus stalls selling jewellery and accessories. The people-watching is first-class – there's a lot of dressing up. Tickets go on sale about six weeks before the fair, but are usually available on the door; a wristband means you can pop in and out through the afternoon and so make use of the many food options nearby.

Watch the boats go by
Great River Race

> greatriverrace.org.uk

Described by the organisers as 'London's River Marathon', this fabulous flotilla is a stirring sight. More than 300 vessels (fixed-seat only) race the 21.6 miles from Millwall to Ham, powered only by oars or paddles. Crews come from all over the world, some out to win, others competing for charity or just the joy of taking part. Much of the fun for spectators is the sheer variety of boats, with entries including everything from canoes and skiffs to Chinese dragon boats and Cornish gigs. It's the most entertaining race on the river. Choose your vantage point along the route and cheer on the teams of sea scouts, Thames watermen and amateur enthusiasts battling it out for a total of 36 trophies. **The Great River Race** is held annually on a Saturday in September and the start time varies according to the tide. Check the website for details.

> *Entries open in early April*

Meet the people behind the microphones
London Podcast Festival

> kingsplace.co.uk

See village cricket transplanted to Lord's
Voneus Village Cup Final

> nationalvillagecup.com

The year 2025 sees the tenth edition of this annual celebration of all things podcast, held in the second week in September. The line-up since the inaugural festival in 2016 reads like a who's who of podcasting: *My Dad Wrote a Porno, The Rest Is History, Griefcast, Have you Heard George's Podcast?, No Such Thing as a Fish* and *This Paranormal Life* are just some of the hundreds of podcasts that have featured. Held over ten days, it's a chance for fans to see the people behind their favourite shows, hear unique collaborations between podcasters, listen to talks and Q&A sessions and watch podcasts being recorded live. Podcasts often get special guest interviewees for the occasion – Hollywood director Paul Feig, columnist Caitlin Moran and actor Jason Isaacs have all appeared in person, which adds an extra thrill to proceedings.

Each summer, across hundreds of Britain's village greens, thousands of people take part in cricket matches. What do they dream of? If not the dizzy heights of playing for England, perhaps at least playing at Lord's, in the annual final of the **National Village Cup** tournament. The competition has been taking place since 1972, with close to 400 clubs battling through the summer months for the chance to play in the final at Lord's. Seeing the two clubs who make it – in 2023, first-time finalists Milford Hall against Leeds & Broomfield – slug it out in a usually thrilling 50 overs at the home of the game is a real treat. Match play is supplemented by a range of family-friendly activities during the day, including a village fete.

> *Tickets on sale in June*

> *Tickets on sale in August*

SEP

121

Enjoy the arts along London's river
Totally Thames

> totallythames.org

For 28 years, this month-long festival dedicated to London's great waterway and its ecology has been entertaining locals and visitors alike with a consistently creative and diverse programme of events. Most come from the arena of art and culture, and all are centred around the river, with live performances, boating events, art installations, talks, river races and workshops forming the bulk of the activities. In events like river clean-ups, foreshore guided walks, a climate cabaret and immersive, interactive exhibitions highlighting the fragility of our planet, the festival's growing focus on sustainability and protecting the environment and ecosystem of the river are evident. Last year five weekend festival hubs in different riverside locations – Brentford, The Royal Docks, London Bridge, Greenwich and Kingston upon Thames – brought activities to a wider audience than ever, while the return of the parallel Great River Race and St Katharine Docks Classic Boats Festival drew thousands of spectators to their family-friendly days.

> *For the Great River Race, see page 120*

Swoon over sculpture in Regent's Park and beyond
Frieze Sculpture and London Sculpture Week

> frieze.com; sculptureinthecity.org.uk

Each September, Regent's Park is transformed into an Instagrammer's paradise with the arrival of around 20 pieces of outdoor art; yes, **Frieze Sculpture** has come to town – or more accurately, the southernmost reaches of the park, where for a month from mid-September to late-October the pieces delight and bemuse park users who come to relax, eat their lunchtime sandwiches or do a double take as they jog by, with the emphasis on the playful yet insightful. In 2023, Tony Matelli's *Sleepwalker* (2014), Hank Willis Thomas's *All Power to All People* (2023) and British Trinidadian artist Zak Ové's colourful totem pole *The Mothership Connection* (2021) were just some of the great examples of an intelligent selection policy that encompasses the humorous, political and fun, ensuring an enjoyable and thoughtful experience whether you're into art or not. In recent years the event has been joined by London Sculpture Week, SculptureFest, and free guided walking tours.

Ready, Set, Go . . .
Chelsea Flower Show Ticket Registration

> rhs.org.uk

Tickets for what's generally regarded as the world's most prestigious flower show go on sale from the third week of this month. Members of the Royal Horticultural Society (RHS) get first dibs during a week-long window, with sales opening to everyone else a week later. If you're into horticulture, it's worth considering RHS membership, not least because the half-day tickets, at half the price of the full-day ticket, sell out fast, and because membership gets you and a guest unlimited entry to its five wonderful RHS gardens.

> *For Chelsea Flower Show, see page 64*
> *For RHS Hampton Court Palace Garden Festival, see page 96*

Listen to some heated debates in a tent
How the Light Gets In

> howthelightgetsin.org

Held in tents erected on the lawns in front of Hampstead Heath's Kenwood House, the world's largest philosophy and music festival brings together big thinkers across multiple fields of modern culture, philosophy and criticism; in 2023 these included Alastair Campbell, Michio Kaku, Rory Stewart, David Baddiel and Ruby Wax. Alongside debates and round-table discussions, music, comedy, cabaret, and banquets combine to create a site filled with the exchange of ideas,

thought and memorable moments, not least in the Woodburner tent, where intimate performances by acts like Badly Drawn Boy bring each day's events to a nicely chilled-out close. A long-running sister festival takes place each May in Hay-on-Wye, where the event originated in 2018, should you feel the need for more philosophical debate and engagement in an even more bucolic setting than Hampstead Heath.

Share a magical moment at King's Cross station
Back to Hogwarts Day

> **wizardingworld.com**

Let's face it, train stations are generally not magical places. And King's Cross station is no exception. But, every year on 1 September, the north London transport hub is filled with hundreds of Potterheads, who gather to hear the once-a-year announcement of the Hogwarts Express departing from Platform 9¾ for the famed wizarding school. Costumed 'witches and wizards' wait for the 11 a.m. announcement of the train's departure, which, of course, as mere 'muggles' they can't actually see. They do get to see a special board displaying the train's departure, and lots of Harry Potter-related activities make the whole morning huge fun. In the past these have included the chance to enjoy some Butterbeer, play Hogwarts Legacy on a PlayStation5 and take part in photo opportunities, with some lucky fans winning Harry Potter LEGO in giveaways. Activities continue for a day or two after the train's departure, especially if it's a weekend.

Walk through a smile or down a poured staircase
London Design Festival

> londondesignfestival.com

Since it began more than 20 years ago, one of the charms of the **London Design Festival** has been the way it transforms not just one part of the capital, but what feels like the whole of it. Held in various locations such as the V&A, and 'design districts' that stretch from Brompton Road and Chelsea in London to Canary Wharf and Greenwich Peninsula in the east, the festival fills normally grey urban environments with unexpected colour, shapes, forms and activities that can't help but make you smile, think and often get hands on. It's not uncommon to come across some

ethereally strange or surreal installation, such as architect Alison Brooks' 34 m-long urban pavilion that took the shape of a smile, in Chelsea, or a monumentally imposing sculpture like Faye Greenwood's Designpost, in Walthamstow, or a Poured Staircase that's been turned into a rainbow flow of colour by Ian Davenport in Greenwich. Much of the focus is on design as applied art, making it not only fun to look at but fun to engage and interact with, but themes such as loneliness, isolation and relationships are explored too.

Recurring Events

London has a *lot* of history to enjoy. Much of it is available to experience and explore regularly in places like the Guildhall's Roman Amphitheatre, the Tower of London, Buckingham Palace, the Old Royal Naval College at Greenwich, the London Transport Museum and hundreds more. Some of the capital's history is kept under wraps, and only opened up to the public occasionally. Here are a few of popular favourites. For more, sign up to the excellent newsletter at ianvisits.co.uk.

London's Mail Rail tunnel walks

> Various locations; postalmuseum.org

Run by London's Postal Museum, these regular walks offer the chance to learn about the city's 100-year-old postal railway service via its tunnels. Lasting around 75 minutes, walkers are escorted through the original tunnels, tracks and station platforms by a guide who'll offer fascinating titbits from its history – like how the spaces were used during the First World War to store and protect national art treasures.

King's Observatory

> Richmond Park; kingsobservatory.co.uk

A library, two octagonal rooms lined with their original plywood, Chinese and Japanese ceramics collection and, the *piece de resistance*, a tiny telescope observatory cuppola built for and used by George III are just some of the highlights of this eighteenth-century Palladian house in the middle of the Royal Mid-Surrey Golf Club in Richmond Park. Just watch out for those golf balls. Fore!

Charterhouse by Candelight

> The City; thecharterhouse.org; winter months

There are guided tours of the medieval monastery, great hall and courtyards of the Tudor mansion that make up Charterhouse's heritage site throughout the year (as well as other specialist tours, including a garden tour and art and interiors tour). In the winter months, however, the chance to explore its 600+ years of history takes on a new light as all its nooks and crannies, seventeenth-century portraits and beautiful Norfolk cloister are lit only by flickering candlelight. A pop-up bar serves drinks before the hour-long tour, with the Great Chamber and bar remaining open for an hour afterwards.

Crossness Pumping Station open days and guided tours

> Abbey Wood, Bexley; crossness.org.uk

Known as the Cathedral on the Marsh, the Victorian Crossness pumping station is a treat to behold, and once a month, the Prince Consort Engine, one of its four original steam engines, is switched on for visitors. More regular guided tours of the site offer insights into how the station helped end London's sewage problems. The station's north river counterpart, the gloriously gothic Abbey Mills pumping station near West Ham, can sometimes be visited during Open House (see page 118).

Cosmic House

> Holland Park; jencksfoundation.org;
> three times a week

Fans of garden design will be familiar with the name of Charles Jencks, the landscape designer and co-founder of the Maggie's Cancer Care Centres, but perhaps not with his London home in Holland Park. Yet the early postmodern design of its interior is just as extraordinary as Jencks's garden design, and it's open to small groups three afternoons a week throughout much of the year.

LT Museum Hidden London tours

> Various locations; ltmuseum.co.uk; year round

Whether it's the eight deep-level underground shelters of Clapham South, one of London's first Underground stations at Moorgate, the disused platforms at Charing Cross or, perhaps best of all, the abandoned platforms, tunnels and ticket hall of the terminus at Aldwych, London Transport Museum's Hidden London tours are all winners.

Banqueting House tours

> Whitehall, Westminster; hrp.org.uk;
> one day a month

Tours of Inigo Jones's 1622 Banqueting House, built for James I and wife Anne of Denmark, and the site of Charles I's execution, are held throughout the year (usually three tours on one day a month). Lasting around an hour, they offer a chance to see the crowning glory of the building, a carved and gilded ceiling featuring the only in situ paintings by Flemish artist Rubens, probably commissioned by Charles I. For other great examples of Jones's work, Somerset House on the Strand and The Queen's House in Greenwich are accessible year-round.

Old Royal Naval College dome tours

> Greenwich; ornc.org;
> March to October

Twice a week between March and October, the dome of Sir Christopher Wren's Old Royal Naval College in Greenwich is opened up to six visitors at a time. The 125-step climb brings you out to a soaring space filled with light and far-reaching views, as well as the opportunity to see the inner workings of the historic turret clock above the Chapel and learn about the history of the space.

St Alfege Greenwich tours

> Greenwich; st-alfege.org.uk;
> alternate Saturday mornings

Every other Saturday morning there's the chance to visit the crypt and galleries of this church built on the site where St Alfege was killed by the Danes in 1012 AD. A tour of the present church, dating from the early eighteenth century and designed by Nicholas Hawksmoor, takes in some of that thousand-year history, as well as its hidden spaces, including the vaults and a suspended ceiling that was the largest in Europe when the church was built.

Heritage Open days

> Various locations; heritageopendays.org.uk;
> September

For ten days every September, many of London's heritage buildings and sites are opened to the public for free. A wide range of absorbing activities includes curator and conservationist talks, concerts, guided tours and walks, free London vintage bus rides and heaps of workshops and classes – such as stained glass and medieval dancing.

Wilton's Music Hall guided history tours

> Tower Hill; wiltons.org.uk;
> a few times per month

The tiny Wilton's Music Hall has been many things in its 300-year existence, including a home, shop, sailors' pub, Mission and, in 1859, the Victorian Music Hall we can view today behind the row of buildings on Graces Alley. Seeing a performance here is a treat, but to really get into the nooks and crannies of the site, a guided hour-long tour, held a few times each month, is a must.

Nunhead Cemetery guided tours

> Peckham; fonc.org.uk; throughout the year

This magnificent south-east London cemetery – indeed one of London's original Magnificent Seven garden cemeteries – has a fascinating range of tours, organised by the Friends of Nunhead Cemetery, throughout the year. And they're free, though it would be churlish not to offer a donation to ensure their work can continue. General tours lasting ninety minutes to two hours are held regularly. Some specialist events occur less frequently, including woodland walks, cemetery symbol walks and music hall artistes' walks.

Guildhall monthly tours

> City of London; cityoflondonguides.com

The regular guided tours of this stately fourteenth-century building offer the chance to learn about famous events that have taken place in its impressive spaces, but also something more; held on the days when there's a Common Council meeting in session, participants can attend the meetings after their tour to see the City's democracy in action. The City of London Guides, who run the tours, also offer Old Bailey Tours and City of London walking tours.

Tour of Lincoln's Inn

> Holborn; incolnsinn.org.uk; weekly

Ninety-minute tours of Lincoln's Inn, whose collection of legal buildings dates back at least 600 years, are held weekly, and take in everything from its seventeenth-century chapel and an eighteenth-century set of chambers to the Great Hall complex, opened by Queen Victoria in 1845 and featuring a fresco by G.F. Watts. An impressive art collection includes works by leading lights such as William Hogarth, Sir Joshua Reynolds, Sir Thomas Lawrence, Mary Beale and John Singer Sargent.

An Evening with the Stars at the Royal Observatory

> Greenwich; rmg.co.uk; winter months

Running in the winter months only and over just a handful of dates, this opportunity to explore the night sky (with the help of astronomers) using both modern-day telescopes and the 130-year-old Great Equatorial Telescope of the Royal Observatory is always extremely popular, so book early. Tickets are released in the autumn (usually around September). It all kicks off with a planetarium show and lasts around two hours.

Hampton Court Palace Garden Open Days

> Hampton Court; hrp.org.uk;
  specific days free

The 800+ acres of gardens surrounding Hampton Court can be visited year-round with a palace entry ticket, but on selected days during the year they're opened up for free, with no ticket required. You'll still need to pay if you want to enter the palace, or the maze, but the kitchen garden, great fountain garden and Privy Garden are just some of the gorgeous spaces you can enjoy without having to pay a bean.

Thames Barrier test closures

> Woolwich; gov.uk; monthly

The engineering feat that is the Thames Barrier may be more than 40 years old, but its 10 steel gates spanning 520 metres across the River Thames near Woolwich are still an impressive sight. When they're closed, they offer essential flood protection from tidal surges to 125 square kilometres of central London. Usually open, the gates are closed around once a month for maintenance and test purposes and visitors can see how they work. It's fascinating and free, too. Do call the day before a closure is scheduled to check it's going ahead.

Birdwatching at Woodberry Wetlands,
page 144

October

Celebrate Black heritage
Black History Month

> blackhistorymonth.org.uk

Inspired by **Black History Month** in the USA, the UK BHM is a celebration of Black heritage and culture and promotes tolerance, equality and better race relations. It is held in October (the US version runs in February), and was started in 1987. Journalist and pan-African activist Akyaaba Addai-Sebo, who was working for the GLC (Greater London Council) at the time, saw a need to celebrate, and to educate people about the importance of African and Black culture. Today, BHM includes all sorts of events, in venues ranging from local libraries to major museums –exhibitions, talks, film festivals, music, community parties and more. In 2023,

the focus was on the 75th anniversary of the arrival of the HMT *Empire Windrush*, and the contributions and achievements of Black women to our society – from Mary Seacole, the pioneering British-Jamaican nurse, to contemporary businesswoman Dame Sharon White and long-standing MP Diane Abbott. Typical of the events were photographic exhibitions ('Celebrating Wandsworth's Sheroes' and '*Windrush* Elders') commissioned by Wandsworth Council and shown at Battersea Arts Centre, and the ceremony to unveil a Blue Plaque to anti-racism activist Claudia Jones in Vauxhall, south-west London.

Sit back and listen to the storytellers
London Literature Festival (LLF)

> southbankcentre.co.uk

Held over 10 days at the Southbank Centre, the **London Literature Festival** celebrates the written and spoken word. It attracts international names – Yu Miri and Teju Cole – alongside homegrown talent, such as George the Poet, Ian Rankin, Lemn Sissay and Jacqueline Wilson, but there's also space for up-and-coming writers. Actors who have turned to writing, like Tom Hanks (pictured), Jada Pinkett Smith, Patrick Stewart and Kerry Washington (all of whom have produced memoirs), sprinkle a little stardust on the occasion. Since 2023, the Black British Book Festival has been part of the LLF. It showcases the best of British Black authors and emerging talent. Poetry is also a strength – the National Poetry Library, the largest public collection of modern poetry in the world – is housed at the South Bank Centre. Although the headline acts are ticketed and sell out quickly, many of the events are free, notably ones aimed at young children.

OCT

> *Tickets on sale in early July*

Get crafting
Knitting & Stitching Show

> theknittingandstitchingshow.com

Held over four days in mid-October, **The Knitting & Stitching Show** is London's largest crafts fair, with more than 250 stalls. Exhibitors go from big-name sewing machine companies to individual designer/makers, with a whole range of craft suppliers in the mix. Crochet, knitting, quilting, embroidery, felting, macramé and sewing are all covered, and it's a great place to shop for hard-to-find materials and tools. Some businesses offer special discounts, and if stallholders aren't too busy, they're happy to chat and offer advice. There's also inspiration in the form of exhibitions (the textile degree graduate show is always worth seeing), demonstrations and workshops – pre-bookable classes range from one to three hours, and run from beginner to expert.

Help to celebrate a favourite fruit
Apple Days

Catch real American Football in action
NFL

> nfl.com

Every October, London gets a little taste of the countryside with various apple-based festivities. Fulham Palace hosts an annual **Apple Day**, with a food and drink market, children's garden games and a celebration of their orchard harvest. In Hampstead, the National Trust's Fenton House, site of a 300-year-old orchard, holds an apple weekend during which old varieties of English apple can be sampled. More apple-based activities can be found in the orchards at Valence House in Dagenham and in Dulwich Village. Kentish Town City Farm offers apple-bobbing, apple-pressing and a competition for the longest peel, while Horsenden Farm, in west London, has a craft market with folk music and plenty of apple-based fun. Lots of small community gardens run their own events, so look out for local listings in October. Some years, theatre troupe Lions Part stages an October Plenty, celebrating the fruitful harvest (including apples) and featuring a Corn Queene draped in wheat, fruit and vegetables and culminating in festivities in Borough Market – cider and apple juice are involved.

America's **National Football League** began playing regular games internationally in 2005, and the first game came to London in 2007. Over the years since then almost 40 games have been staged in London, featuring teams such as the New York Giants, the Seattle Seahawks and the Dallas Cowboys. 2024 saw two League games played at Tottenham Hotspur Stadium, where the football pitch is magically transformed into an NFL field. The number of games may increase in future years as the NFL is keen to expand its global reach. In a separate initiative, the Jacksonville Jaguars have played a home game in London since 2012 – they are scheduled to play at Wembley Stadium. There's lots of fun, family-friendly activities based around the action, which happens in early October.

OCT

> *Twelfth Night, also Lions Part, see page 20.*

> *Tickets on sale in June*

Stock up on beauty at an anti-Frieze event
The Other Art Fair

> theotherartfair.com

Let's go fly a kite!
Kite Day on Blackheath

> blackheath.org

One of London's art establishment big-ticket events is, of course, Frieze, but its early focus on wealth and big name galleries meant that the capital's indie art scene didn't get much of a look-in. The **Other Art Fair** was set up to give a presence to the alternative spaces that make up that scene. It's now so successful that it's held twice a year, usually for a week in mid-October, and again in March, at Brick Lane's vast Old Truman Brewery. The focus is on art for sale at all price points, with work from more than 120 artists shown in a vibrant atmosphere, enlivened in no small part by immersive installations, performances, DJs, a fully stocked bar and some imaginative design and creative elements; in 2023's autumn edition, the cavernous space was transformed into a seventies' themed 'Soho-style neon extravaganza' by Walthamstow-based neon art group Gods Own Junkyard (pictured), while 2024's spring fair offered the opportunity to sketch members of the East London Strippers Collective in a life drawing workshop. The Affordable Art Fair, similarly championing work from smaller galleries and artists, also takes place this month.

Each year, the Blackheath Society puts on this lovely event, inviting kite flyers of all ages, experience and abilities to bring their kites to the expansive Heath, where they can watch their birds, dragons, cats, frogs, spacemen, rockets and myriad other wonderful, colourful forms hopefully soar in the skies. Even if you don't have a kite, the day's event is huge fun, thanks in no small part to the annual presence of the Kent Kite Flyers, who bring big, spectacular kites to fly in the specially set up arena and are on hand to give help and advice. A steel band from the local Grinling Gibbons School in Deptford adds a fun performance element, and food and non-alcoholic drinks are also on hand.

Up, up and away ...
The Lord Mayor's Hot Air Balloon Regatta

> balloonregatta.com

Seeing up to 50 hot air balloons cross the skies of London is a magical sight – and these days, a very rare one. As the aerial extension of the historic Lord Mayor's Show, the fundraising event for the Lord Mayor's Appeal has bags of its own appeal, and dates back to 1992, when Sir Brian Jenkins, accompanied by Lady Jenkins, became the first Lord Mayor to fly across the City of London in a hot air balloon – one of twelve that flew that morning. These days the event often falls victim to the vagaries of the British weather and hasn't actually taken place since 2019. At time of writing, the 2024 event is planned, with standby dates in place in case of short-notice cancellation. So keep your eyes on the skies – and more importantly, on the website, where updates will be posted re planned dates and changes.

Enjoy a properly grown-up Halloween
Adult Halloween events

> londonmonthofthedead.com

With its growing commercialisation, it's easy to forget that Halloween is actually a celebration of All Saints Day, or the Day of Dead, when people remember loved ones they've lost. London's cemeteries mark the period with a range of wonderfully engaging and appropriate walks, talks and more. To find them, check out the individual cemeteries' websites in the months leading up to October, or the London Month of the Dead website. This imaginative organisation puts on a range of great events across many of London's cemeteries during October. Whether you choose to join a Halloween Folklore Walk at Nunhead Cemetery, speak Shakespeare's Ghosts in a two-hour voice workshop in and around Brompton Cemetery's chapel, take a lantern-lit tour among the tombs of Tower Hamlets Cemetery Park, join a mouse taxidermy workshop in Kensal Green Cemetery, learn about the architecture of death in Highgate Cemetery or enjoy a candlelit theramin concert in Brompton Cemetery, you'll have an unforgettable Halloween.

> *Tickets on sale in July*

OCT

Celebrate the best of global cinema
BFI London Film Festival

> whatson.bfi.org.uk

Hang with the art glitterati
Frieze London

> frieze.com

From its humble conception in 1956 as a festival dedicated to showing winning films from industry behemoths such as Cannes, Venice and Berlin, via its first outing in 1957, when Akira Kurosawa's *Throne of Blood*, Ingmar Bergman's *The Seventh Seal* and Federico Fellini's *Nights of Cabiria* illustrated the festival's international focus, the two-week long British Film Festival has gone from strength to strength. In 2023, it included more than 60 premieres among its 400+ movies from more than 70 countries, screened across the whole of the capital. With red carpet events galore and an admirable rebalancing of focus on homegrown and emerging talent as much as international stars, the festival offers a great chance to see films you may never get a chance to see elsewhere, thanks to an imaginative programme that always includes lots of films without UK distribution deals. Tickets go on sale to the general public in mid-September, but it's worth considering BFI membership for priority booking, which usually opens a week or so before.

Twenty-something years on and still going strong, Britain's biggest art fair clearly still pulls in the punters, possibly drawn to the two-week long event as much for the celeb sightings – in recent years, Florence Pugh, Rami Malek, Andrew Garfield, FKA Twigs and Jared Leto, to name just a few – as the art. Its clout and influence is undeniable, and its exclusive focus on contemporary art (created mainly post-2000) and living artists always ensures there is work worth seeing, whether it be by the artists of globally recognised galleries such as Hauser & Wirth, White Cube and Sprüth Magers or smaller but influential up-and-coming spaces such as Vardaxoglou. Frieze Masters, which runs concurrently, explores the relationship between historical art and contemporary practice with work made before the year 2000, while the free Frieze Sculpture (see page 123) connects the two spaces across Regent's Park.

> *Tickets on sale in September*

Drink your fill of hearty ale
London Oktoberfest

> london-oktoberfest.co.uk

Beer lovers of the world, don your lederhosen and pack your pretzels, **Oktoberfest** is back in town. The location of the annual beer event moves around the capital but since 2011 the five-day event has become a staple of the London drinking scene, its giant tent filled with music, German food, full Oktoberfest decoration (think gingham tablecloths, fairy lights and waiting staff in dirndl and lederhosen) and, of course, lots and lots of steins of Bavarian beer, specially made for Oktoberfest in a small brewery close to Nuremberg. Weekdays see corporate gatherings, so get your company to sign up if you fancy a day's drinking, singing and dancing with your colleagues, or just head to the tent at the weekend for a fun day with friends.

Dust off the binoculars, it's migration time
Birdwatching

> wildlondon.org.uk

See an art show with a real difference
Koestler Arts Freedom Exhibition

> koestlerarts.org.uk

Autumn migration is in full swing this month, with birds making their long journeys from summer breeding grounds in the north to wintering grounds in the south, and London is a handy stopover point between them. The two most rewarding places to see the birds up close and learn everything about them are west London's huge London Wetland Centre and north-east London's Walthamstow Wetlands, where you're sure to see many types of wintering geese and ducks. The occasional sighting of more unusual varieties, such as green sandpipers, black-tailed godwits, greenshank, shoveler, gadwall, redwings and stonechats, add extra brownie points. Details of recent sightings, information panels, webcams and numerous hides make spotting birds in these places a doddle. At the smaller 11-hectare Woodberry Wetlands in Stoke Newington, breeding kingfishers add flashes of iridescent beauty. Grab a table on the top floor or terrace of the Coal House Café and settle in with those binoculars for some rare and wonderful sights and flights. And even if you don't spot many birds, the rich autumn colours of such special London sites make time spent in them endlessly rewarding.

The Koestler Awards art exhibition has been taking place at the Southbank Centre since 2008, and has been around way longer than that, having celebrated its 60th anniversary in 2022. But many people have never heard of it. Which is a shame, because with wonderfully original and inventive work on display, it's one of the most fascinating and different exhibitions you're likely to see in London. Bringing together hundreds of works by people in prisons, secure mental health facilities, immigration removal centres, young offender institutions and on community sentences across the UK, it acts as a great showpiece for the work done by the Koestler Arts charity, which was set up to inspire prisoners and people with experience of the criminal justice system to take part in the arts. Usually opening in mid-October and on display until December, each annual exhibition is curated by one person, from families of prisoners and victims of crime to some of the arts' biggest names – in 2024 Jeremy Deller and John Conti shared the role, with past curators including Antony Gormley, Benjamin Zephaniah and Sarah Lucas.

Run the Royal parks
Royal Parks Half Marathon

> royalparkshalf.com

If a full marathon seems beyond your imagination/capabilities/endurance, this excellent alternative may be much more palatable. Held each October, it offers the chance to run half the marathon distance (13.1-miles) within four of London's eight Royal Parks – Hyde Park, The Green Park, St James's Park and Kensington Gardens. Originally set up as an annual fundraising initiative to help conserve and enhance the 5,000 acres that make up London's eight Royal Parks, it also raises money for 1,200 other charities of all sizes, with runners able to choose who they raise funds for. Entry is similar to the London Marathon, with a first ballot in January, the chance to enter a second ballot in February or the possibility of running for a charity, which offers guaranteed entry. Want to run with work colleagues against other companies? Get your company to consider entering the Royal Bank of Canada Corporate 13.1 race.

> *Ballot opens in January*

OCT

145

An autumn colour walk
(Epping Forest), p156

November

Watch a stately procession
State Opening of Parliament

> parliament.uk

The most ceremonial event in the parliamentary calendar, the **State Opening** happens on the first day of a new parliamentary session (or shortly after a general election). It moves around the calendar, but often takes place in November. It's the only regular occasion when the three parts of Parliament – the Sovereign, the House of Lords and the House of Commons – meet. The monarch reads out a speech written by the government, outlining their agenda for the coming session. The best bit, as far as pageantry goes, is the procession from Buckingham Palace to Westminster, escorted by the Household Cavalry. At 11 a.m., the Irish State Coach sets off carrying the King, following another coach holding the royal regalia – the Imperial State Crown, the Cap of Maintenance and Sword of State. The route goes along the Mall, through Horse Guards Parade, down Whitehall and then Parliament Street, arriving at the Palace of Westminster at 11.15 a.m.

Pay your respects to those fallen in war
Remembrance Sunday

> britishlegion.org.uk

Listen to jazz from around the globe
EFG London Jazz Festival

> efglondonjazzfestival.org.uk

The **Remembrance Day** ceremony is held on the Sunday nearest to 11 November – day the First World War ended in 1918. It's a sombre occasion that honours those from Britain and the Commonwealth who died fighting in the world wars and later conflicts. The King, the Prime Minister and various other dignitaries lay wreaths at the Cenotaph on Whitehall. A two-minute silence is followed by a short (25-minute) service of remembrance, and a march past by thousands of ex-service personnel, featuring everyone from the Royal Engineers Bomb Disposal Association and the British Nuclear Test Veterans to the Munitions Workers Association. The public can watch the ceremony from the pavements along Whitehall and Parliament Street – access starts at 8 a.m. There are video screens dotted around nearby. Check the website for details.

The **London Jazz Festival** started in 1992, and now has over 300 shows across more than 70 venues, featuring musicians from all over the world. The ten-day extravaganza in November is London's largest city-wide music festival and encompasses up-and-coming bands alongside musical legends, across all styles of jazz. Recent years have seen acts ranging from singer Dianne Reeves to Malian kora harp player Ballaké Sissoko and jazz double-bassist Ron Carter perform. Venues run from Hackney's Cafe Oto to the Royal Festival Hall and Cadogan Hall. There are free gigs too, at the Barbican and the South Bank Centre.

NOV

Experience the ultimate in Christmas shopping
Winter Markets

Get into the festive spirit early with a trip to a **winter market**. Some of the most evocative and food-focused markets are Scandinavian. The Finnish and Norwegian churches in Rotherhithe hold a Scandinavian Christmas Fair on two weekends (late November and early December). The Swedish church in Marylebone holds a fair over three days in mid-November. Expect traditional Christmas products and mulled wine. More generic winter markets can be found in central London, notably in Leicester Square and Trafalgar Square, both offering food, drink and Christmas sparkle. The south bank of the Thames is home to two winter markets: one near Waterloo Bridge and another between London and Tower bridges, again both food-centred. The market near Tower Bridge also has pop-up entertainment. There's a maker's market near the London Eye on various Sundays in the run-up to Christmas, too.

> *For the Taste of London, see p.81; for Christmas Fairs & Open Studios, see p.153*

Enjoy one of London's best parades
Lord Mayor's Show

> lordmayorsshow.london

The new Lord Mayor's first full day in office is marked by an entertaining hour-long procession on the second Saturday in November. The route starts from Mansion House at 11 a.m. and runs to the Royal Courts of Justice (the return leg leaves Temple just after 1 p.m. and travels along the Embankment and Queen Victoria Street). It's quite a spectacle: 100 or so floats are joined by horse-drawn carriages, giant inflatables, brass marching bands, military vehicles, heritage buses, Chinese dragons and more. Seeing the different livery companies parade past is fascinating – the Worshipful Company of Basketmakers, for example, wove the giant figures of Gog and Magog (protectors of the City of London), who are part of the procession. The Lord Mayor himself rides in the gilded State Coach. It's a family-friendly occasion and finding a good vantage point is easy. There's lots of music, and the atmosphere is lively but it's not too hectic. What's more, because most of the roads along and around the route are closed to traffic, it's a blissfully car-free day.

NOV

Revel in the beauty of vintage vehicles
London to Brighton Veteran Car Run

> veterancarrun.com

A delightful and surprisingly varied spectacle, with all manner of vintage vehicles taking on the challenge of the 60 miles between London and Brighton. The first **London to Brighton Run** occurred in 1896 and was called the Emancipation Run, to celebrate the lifting of the requirement of a person to walk in front of the vehicle with a red flag, and the raising of the speed limit from 4mph to 14mph. These days, car names include the familiar – Daimler, Peugeot – and the less well known – De Dion Bouton, Pick. You may see an 1898 Leon Bollee, a tandem two-seater from France, Wolseleys and Royal Enfields from the UK or a 1903 Cadillac from the States, plus a sprinkling of motorbikes and bicycles. The race starts at 7 a.m., from Serpentine Road, Hyde Park, and finishes on Madeira Drive in Brighton, where vehicles start to arrive from 10 a.m. – though the slower ones arrive through the afternoon. Many of the cars can also be seen on show in St James's the day before the race. Check the website for details of this and the full race route.

Shop for curated gifts in special surroundings
Christmas Fairs & Open Studios

The best **Christmas fairs** are a classy way to festive shop, and usually sell a range of goods by designer-makers, alongside items sold for good causes. Look out for them from November onwards. The Guildhall Christmas Market benefits the British Red Cross and is their largest fundraising event; the historic surroundings add to the festive atmosphere. Charterhouse Christmas Fair in Clerkenwell is worth going to for the setting alone, as are the Beautiful & Useful Craft Fair at the Garden Museum, and the Christmas fairs at Chelsea Physic Garden and Dulwich College, both of which host more than 100 stalls.

The Business Design Centre is less of a lure, but it's the venue for the *Country Living Magazine* Christmas Fair, a behemoth that covers every aspect of the season; the Spirit of Christmas at Olympia is in a similar vein. More intimate is the Selvedge Christmas Fair, run by the textile magazine of the same name, which has a carefully curated roster of stalls selling everything from vintage fabrics to hand-embroidered treasures. Also good for one-off presents are open studio days – Cockpit Studios is home to scores of makers/artists and opens its doors to the public over a weekend in late November.

NOV

Explore one of London's greatest buildings for free
Open day at St Paul's Cathedral

> stpauls.co.uk

As part of the celebrations marking the Lord Mayor's first day in office, St Paul's Cathedral throws open its doors and welcomes visitors for free (the usual entrance fee, unless you attend a service, at the time of writing costs more than £20). Access to the Dome isn't included, but otherwise visitors have free rein of the magnificent building. As well as the soaring, awe-inspiring architecture and historic artefacts, there are modern works of art such as a sculpture by Henry Moore and video installations by Bill Viola. The large crypt is packed with memorials to the great and the good (not all of them buried here), including Admiral Lord Nelson, Florence Nightingale, Alexander Fleming and Sir Christopher Wren, the cathedral's architect; Winston Churchill is remembered by a set of gates. You might also hear the Grand Organ in action – it's the third largest in the UK, and its case, by Grinling Gibbons, is one of the Cathedral's treasures.

Remember a loved one
Ever After Garden

> royalmarsden.org

Discover a world of sackbuts and serpents
London International Festival of Early Music

> lifem.org

From mid-November to just before Christmas, Grosvenor Square in Mayfair is lit up by more than 25,000 illuminated white roses. The swathe of lights is intended as a garden of remembrance, and all are welcome, but visitors can also choose to dedicate a rose to the memory of a loved one. The garden looks magical, but it also works as a fundraiser. Proceeds go to the Royal Marsden Cancer Charity, which, since 2019, has received hundreds of thousands of pounds from supporters. Inspiration for the Ever After Garden came from the Light Rose Garden, developed by Korean creative group PANCOMMUNICATION, in Seoul, in 2014. The **Ever After Garden** is open 3-9 p.m. daily. For the best effect wait until it's completely dark. It is a moving experience, as well as a visual pleasure.

For three days in mid-November, the wonderfully eccentric **London International Festival of Early Music** (or the more manageable LIFEM), brings the world of ancient music to Blackheath Halls in southeast London. It's been a staple of the capital's classical music scene since 1973, when it was held at the Royal College of Music, and its mix of live events and exhibition offers a fascinating insight into a world in which crumhorns, cornamuses, shawms, gemshorns, sackbuts, serpents, chitarrones, theorbos and vihuelas are in common usage. Centred around an exhibition of these – and many more – early music instruments, LIFEM's programme of performances, makers' demonstration recitals, workshops, talks and festival evensong attracts makers, professionals, amateurs and early-music lovers to hear both old and new works for early music instruments. The premier of an annual commission for a new piece is the undoubted star of the show. In 2024, award-winning Dutch recorder virtuoso and musicologist Erik Bosgraaf stepped in as the festival's artistic director, hopefully ushering in even more new directions and fans.

NOV

Leaf your cares behind
Autumn Walks

Forget planet-unfriendly long-haul flights to New England. With around 20 per cent of London consisting of public green space, the capital is one of the best cities in the world in which to become an autumn leaf peeper. To the west, Richmond Park's 2,500 acres is filled with fiery reds and oranges, particularly in the 40-acre Isabella Plantation, where the acers reflect beautifully in three ponds. In central London, colourful reflections in the lake of St James's Park are equally dazzling, with the turrets of Horse Guards adding a fairytale dimension to the landscape, while Regent's Park and, heading east, Epping Forest and Greenwich Park are other great spots for autumn colour. But for sheer scale, nothing compares to Kew Gardens, where the Treetop Walkway offers unique views of the autumn leaves and the autumnal colours are beautifully reflected in the waters of the lake.

Watch London twinkle
Christmas Lights & Window Displays

Oxford and Regent streets are the big hitters when it comes to Christmas lights, but Carnaby Street comes a close second in terms of OTT visual impact. Other main shopping streets, such as Bond Street and Marylebone High Street, are reliable destinations for festive bling, and Covent Garden, particularly around the Piazza, is a twinkly delight. A walk along the South Bank from the Royal Festival Hall to London Bridge is recommended, too: many of the buildings are specially illuminated, including the Globe Theatre and the Shard. London's department stores provide smaller scale doses of Christmas loveliness: if you only see one display, make it Fortnum & Mason, where not just the windows but the entire store façade is brilliantly decorated, but Liberty, Selfridges and Harrods also enchant. Smaller shops with a strong design aesthetic, ranging from Hermès (high-end accessories) to Choosing Keeping (exquisite stationery and, at Christmas-time, tree decorations) are also worth seeking out.

NOV

Spook the kids
Childrens' Halloween Events

> timeout.com

Falling as it does at the start of half term, there are myriad Halloween activities around the city for little ones, including ghostly bus tours, wizard afternoon teas and special events at historical sites such as Hampton Court and the Tower of London. You can find many of the best ones in spaces that aren't all about making money. These include many of the city's lovely farms, such as Mudchute, which offers spooky dressing up and pumpkin carving competitions, and Stepney, where kids can make Halloween masks, lanterns and pumpkins. The London Wetlands Centre too is always a good place to head, and has a themed interactive trail, while the Horniman Museum's Halloween Fair goes to town with a fancy dress parade, themed arts and craft activities (slime making workshop, anyone?), spooky magicians and even a Halloween Disco. London listings website *Time Out* usually offers a great round-up of activities and events for both adults and kids close to the big day.

Trip the light fantastic
Christmas Light Trails

In winter, the thousands of trees across London's many green spaces and gardens take on an ethereally skeletal beauty but from November to January, some of these spaces become something else altogether. Employing a multitude of illumination techniques from simple fairy lights and LEDs to lasers and holograms, paths become rainbows of colour and borders, lawns, ponds and trees are filled with water installations, interactive displays, twinkling light tunnels and bright hues. Kew Gardens has the most famous with a trail of more than 3 km featuring, in 2024, three-metre high illuminated flowers, cascading lights suspended from the tree canopy and a 'Fire Garden' lighting up the Temperate House. At a growing number of other sites, including Eltham Palace, Kenwood House, Syon Park and Hampton Court Palace, light trails transform the natural world into similarly magical, mystical fairytale lands. Hampstead Heath's 1.5 km light trail features millions of twinkling lights, and at Eltham, the 2 km light trail has in the past incorporated holographic talking birds in ornate cages, torchlit gardens, and projections onto the walls of the palace. Check local press near the time for more festive light trails.

NOV

Walk in a winter wonderland
Hyde Park Winter Wonderland

> hydeparkwinterwonderland.com

We may not often get snow in London, but for six weeks from November to January, we do get a **winter wonderland**. The undoubted centrepiece is a funfair featuring more than 15 classic rides which in the past have included four rollercoasters – among them the twistastic Wilde Mause and the five sky-high breathtaking loops of the Munich Looping – a drop tower, wave swinger and high G-force pendulum ride XXL, alongside a range of funhouses and more gentle family-friendly rides such as the Christmas tree ride.

Many of the funhouses and smaller rides are Christmas and snow-themed, ensuring that all ages are catered for, and the self-contained Santaland will have little ones wide-eyed as they're transported to the North Pole and Santa's Grotto via the Santaland Express. Plenty of food and drink options plus two seasonal shows to choose from could keep your here for hours. Just park your inner Grinch at the entrance and you'll have a ball, whatever your age.

Light up your life
Bonfire Night Displays

> visitlondon.com

Guy Fawkes Night fireworks displays – marking the attempt by Guy Fawkes and co to blow up the Houses of Parliament and King James I in the Gunpowder Plot of 5 November 1605 – used to be common in London's parks, but financial constraints, the Pandemic and other factors now mean just a handful still deliver the glorious eye-popping and ear-bashing whooshes, crackles and fizzes of Crosettes, spiders, Roman candles and Japanese Kamuru. One of the best is Alexandra Palace, thanks to the elevated vantage points but also for a range of other activities including, in 2023, a German beer festival, DJ sets, an ice disco and a dazzling light show. If you're climate-conscious, you might want to check if Wimbledon Park is repeating its fire and light show or holding its usual bonfire, but if you must have the real thing, Chiswick Park, Morden Park, Battersea Park, Beckenham, Barnes, Ealing Cricket Club, Walthamstow Cricket Tennis and Squash Club, Brent and Harrow and Kempton Park Racecourse are the places to head.

NOV

Aladdin at the Hackney Empire,
page 166

December

Drink your fill of Victorian Christmas spirit
Dennis Severs' House

> dennissevershouse.co.uk

Get into the Christmas spirit with a festive run
Santa Runs

> santainthecity.co.uk

This evocative Grade II-listed Georgian house in the heart of Spitalfields is a wonderful experience any time of the year, thanks to the dedication of its late owner Dennis Severs, who, on moving from California to London in 1967, made it his life's work to tell the history and changing fortunes of the house through generations of one imaginary family. Since Severs opened the house to the public, in 1980, it has welcomed thousands of visitors who during fascinating – and sometimes candlelit – tours learn about the intriguing history of London's oldest neighbourhood. From late November to early January the house is given a magical makeover for the festive season. In come the likes of a black swan as a table centrepiece, myriad glass decorations, gorgeous natural garlands and wreaths, handmade paper chains and of course Christmas trees, all brought to life with the kinds of smells, colours and lighting that make you feel you've genuinely gone back as much as three hundred years – this year the house celebrated its three hundredth birthday. Tickets for the Christmas period sell out quickly, so register for the house's newsletter to be in with a chance of getting one.

Each year in the run-up to Christmas many of London's parks fill with a very peculiar sight as thousands of runners dressed as Santa Claus take part in **Santa Runs**. Some of the biggest in the past few years have been the 4k Santa in the City run, set around Tate Modern, and runs in Battersea Park, Wimbledon Common, the Olympic Park and Victoria Park, where 5k and 10k options are on offer, along with a Santa costume for all entrants. In the past, runners have also been encouraged to be inventive with their own festive-themed costumes, with prizes on offer for the best in adults, kids and pets categories. For the little ones, a free mini-Santa Run takes place just before the main race. Registration usually opens a few months before the events, but charity spaces are often available after registration has closed, or spaces filled.

Bring Christmas cheer to the oldest continuously swum race in the world
Peter Pan Cup

> serpentineswimmingclub.com

Every Christmas morning, the cold, murky waters of Hyde Park's Serpentine Lake are broken by hundreds of members of the Serpentine Swimming Club, who race over 100 yards for the Peter Pan Cup (so-called after author J.M. Barrie became associated with the race in 1903, when he donated the cup). These doughty souls – more than 80 of whom have completed successful solo English Channel swims – are permitted by the Royal Parks to swim in the lake every morning, and have been doing so year-round since the club's founding in 1864. A race is held every Saturday morning, but it's the 100-yard Christmas day race, thought to be the oldest continuously swum race in the world, that is the most famous and popular. It takes place at 9 a.m., with a bagpipe player kicking things off, so get to the park well before then to bag a good spot and cheer on those club members who've been lucky (or should that be unlucky?) enough to have made the cut.

DEC

Experience a unique Christmas tradition
Christmas Pantomimes

> bigpantoguide.co.uk

Fill your eyes with a feast of Christmas trees
Churchill Arms

> churchillarmskensington.co.uk

A singular oddity of the British Christmas season is the pantomime, and boy, does London know how to go to town on this peculiar form of participatory musical theatre (oh yes it does). Pantomime has a lengthy and fascinating history that dates back to ancient Greece and Italy. In its British form, it's essentially a well-known fairy tale or fable reimagined with song, dance, slapstick comedy, cross-dressing, topical jokes, innuendo, audience interaction and general mayhem. And yet, despite all this joy, laughter and craziness, it's also about the triumph of good over evil. We know going into it that no matter what happens, everything will be OK. All you really need to know to enjoy the experience is that you will HAVE to sing along, chant, respond to the surreal characters and immerse yourself completely in the sheer silliness of it all. Many of London's pantos have featured famous stars, with the likes of Elton John, Lily Savage, Ian McKellen and Priscilla Presley giving it their all as pantomime dames, queens and evil witches, but the Iconic London pantomime features a person who has made the form all his own – Clive Rowe. For almost 20 years the musical star has made the Hackney Empire his home most Christmases, and is, without a doubt, the one person to catch in panto. Oh yes he is.

London's most famous Christmas tree is of course the one that appears annually from the beginning of December in Trafalgar Square. A gift from the city of Oslo since 1947, it acts as a beautiful backdrop to the many charity carol services held under it each year, but standing in solitary splendour, with none of the kinds of Christmas lights you associate with London, it is rather understated. But a few miles west of the square on lovely Kensington Church Street, small corner pub the Churchill Arms really puts on a show when it comes to Christmas trees, covering its façade in late November with up to 100 trees, decorated with thousands of lights. It is an astonishing sight, and sure to melt the heart of the most stubborn bah humbuger. The rest of the year, the pub's frontage is decorated with hundreds of hanging baskets, making it a joy to have a proper London ale in at any time of the year.

Start the year with a bang
New Year's Eve Fireworks

> london.gov.uk

These days the central London firework extravaganza for New Year's Eve is a ticketed event. Tickets go on sale in early November and sell out fast (though there's a second ticket release at the beginning of December). There are six different ticketed viewing areas: Blue (Victoria Embankment from Westminster Bridge to Golden Jubilee Footbridge); Red (Victoria Embankment from Golden Jubilee Footbridge to Temple Avenue); Pink (Waterloo Bridge); Green (behind the London Eye); White (Westminster Bridge); and an accessible viewing area, Orange (Albert Embankment, next to St Thomas's Hospital). You can't move between them, so make sure everyone you hope to meet up with has tickets for the same area. The display is launched from the London Eye at midnight and lasts until 12.30 a.m. It's quite a spectacle, with some of the fireworks shooting up to 200 metres into the sky, allowing people without tickets a glimpse of the pyrotechnics from afar.

Glide into the festive season
Ice Skating

Skating is now fully established as a London winter tradition, and more rinks pop up every year. One of the most beautiful places to skate outdoors is the courtyard at Somerset House; the extravagant Christmas tree is a highlight. Events run from Chilled Out morning slots (with fewer people on the ice) to Skate Lates (DJ nights). Other impressively sited rinks include the one next to Hampton Court Palace, right by the Thames (and over 1,000 sq m) and at Queen's House, Greenwich. The rink at Canary Wharf is set in Canada Square Park and hosts a variety of specials running from old school soul nights to wheelchair sessions. Unlike most outdoor rinks, it is open from October to February. Winter Wonderland in Hyde Park has an ice rink built around a Victorian bandstand. One of the newest skating spots is Glide at Battersea Power Station, which boasts three interconnecting rinks, views of the Thames and a wealth of entertainment.

> *For Winter Wonderland, see page 160*

Watch some of the best equine performers in the world
London International Horse Show

> londonhorseshow.com

Hear a musical range of Yuletide sounds
Christmas Carols and Music

This celebration of horse and rider is held over two arenas at ExCel, in mid-December. Between them, the International Arena and the London Arena host the World Cup qualifiers in Show Jumping, Dressage and Driving, various showing categories (from Middleweight and Heavyweight Hunter to Small Riding Horse), plus displays, masterclasses and even the Kennel Club Dog Agility competitions. There's also a Live Zone, where there are talks, a chance to get autographs from favourite riders and the opportunity to see some of the animals at close quarters. Aside from the competitions, most excitement is generated by the displays. They are different every year, but always stellar: 2023 saw the appearance of the exquisite Portuguese Lusitanos, and also the glorious pageantry of the Musical Drive of the King's Troop Royal Horse Artillery.

> *Tickets on sale in April*

Every cathedral and church organises a carol service at Christmas, but hopeful attendees should plan for the most popular well in advance. The traditional service of Lessons and Carols at St Paul's Cathedral is a ticketed, sell-out performance. It's slightly easier to get tickets for the carol services at churches such as All Souls, Langham Place or St Martin-in-the-Fields; both look beautifully festive. Southwark Cathedral holds candlelit services throughout the year, but look for seasonal treats such as *A Tudor Christmas by Candlelight*; similarly, St James, Piccadilly stages candlelit events. St Bartholomew the Great is a striking church with a list of mostly unticketed services, including German, American and Medieval carol services. The Barbican has a roster of Christmassy musical events, including a Christmas carol singalong, as does the Royal Albert Hall. For something a little different, try the annual service of Jazz Carols at Methodist Central Hall.

Index

About the authors

Yolanda Zappaterra is a London-based author, editor and researcher who has worked on more than thirty books. She writes about architecture, art, design and travel, and contributes regularly to leisure, lifestyle and art and design magazines.

Sarah Guy has written about London – and further afield – for many years, covering everything from restaurants and shops to events and walks. She has also commissioned and edited a range of titles, including travel guides, photography books and essay collections.

Picture credits

Quarto

First published in 2024 by Frances Lincoln
an imprint of The Quarto Group.
One Triptych Place, London, SE1 9SH
United Kingdom
T (0)20 7700 6700
www.Quarto.com

A catalogue record for this book is available from
the British Library.

ISBN 978-0-7112-9335-9
EISBN 978-1-8360-0352-6

10 9 8 7 6 5 4 3 2 1

Book Designer: Masumi Briozzo
Commissioning Editor: John Parton
Editor: Charlotte Frost
Editorial Director: Nicky Hill
Publisher: Philip Cooper
Senior Designer: Isabel Eeles
Production Director: Angela Graef

Printed in China